A Linguistically Inclusive Approach to Grading Writing

A Practical Guide

Hannah A. Franz

Foreword by Vershawn Ashanti Young

TEACHERS COLLEGE PRESS
TEACHERS COLLEGE | COLUMBIA UNIVERSITY
NEW YORK AND LONDON

Published by Teachers College Press,® 1234 Amsterdam Avenue, New York, NY 10027

Front cover photo: Ground Picture / Shutterstock.

Library of Congress Cataloging-in-Publication Data is available at loc.gov

ISBN 978-0-8077-6932-4 (paper)
ISBN 978-0-8077-6933-1 (hardcover)
ISBN 978-0-8077-8220-0 (ebook)

Printed on acid-free paper
Manufactured in the United States of America

Contents

Foreword

In May of 2020, George Floyd was murdered—smack dab during my multiyear role as chair of CCCC (Conference on College Composition and Communication), the largest international organization devoted to the teaching of writing and communication. Mr. Floyd's death is arguably one of the most impactful culture- and education-changing tragedies of our century (Young, 2020; Young, Balester, & Davies, 2021). To fully understand that impact, we must unpack the import and connect our words as educators, linguists, and writing teachers to that tragedy. Considering Mr. Floyd's death, we must speak to truth to our powers. That is, we should speak truth not only to the power structures we resist from without but also to those operating from within our classrooms, in the educational institutions, ideologies, and practices that we support.

By now we all know what happened. Mr. Floyd was murdered by a white male Minneapolis police officer, as three other officers—all male, of various multiracial backgrounds—failed to intervene. The offending officer was found guilty of second-degree murder for pressing his unrelenting knee into Mr. Floyd's neck for 9 minutes and 29 seconds before he muffled out a cry to his momma and then died. The other three officers were found guilty for violating Mr. Floyd's civil rights because they rendered no aid and were thus complicit in their inaction (Levenson, 2021; Silva, 2022).

We must also recall that Darnella Frazier, a girl of only 17, used her mobile phone to capture and publish the brutality that the world witnessed (Triesman, 2021). In so doing, this African American youth set ablaze the world's conscience—particularly, the consciences of educational organizations. The fire did not consume them, but rather brought into the light multiple pronouncements from educational institutions, such as the American Studies Association (2020), National Council of Teachers of Mathematics (2020), and my own organization, CCCC, which is interested in the connection between the teaching of writing and the virulent, unrelenting racism we have witnessed. We asked, what is the correlation, the unspoken cultural relationship? As chair, I commissioned two committees to examine and write a position on cultural racisms, technical and professional communication, and writing studies more broadly. Those committees came through. Their position statements are "This Ain't Another Statement! This is a DEMAND for Black Linguistic Justice!" (Baker-Bell et al., 2020) and "CCCC Black

Technical and Professional Communication Position Statement with Resource Guide." (Mckoy et al., 2020). "This Ain't Another Statement" teases out the violence that occurs against Black and Brown bodies in public streets like Minneapolis and our academic streets, and the "Black Technical" statement excavates and provides resources on how Black expressivity is already a part of technical writing and communication, and can add even more value to field and practice as vestiges of cultural racisms and their linguistic barriers are steadily removed.

I rehearse and bring attention to this history to make this point: CCCC commissions and authorizes position statements, but if I could have commissioned a book for educators of language and writing, broadly construed, it would be Hannah Franz's *A Linguistically Inclusive Approach to Grading Writing: A Practical Guide*. I could and did approve research funding for the precursor project to this book, a project for which Franz is coprincipal investigator with Stanford University linguist Anne Charity Hudley. As Franz writes in her acknowledgments, the CCCC research grant sponsored her joint project with Hudley, which manifested in an invaluable teaching website: the Students' Right to Their Own Writing project (https://charityhudleydickterfranz.com/students-right-to-their-own-writing/). This website is a rich, well-developed resource for writing and assessing writing, speaking directly to students and teachers in guides specifically tailored for them both. Franz's book extends the research there and makes plain and practical how teachers at university, college, and high school levels can teach and importantly assess school-based writing by our students, students who all have accents and who all come from meaningful diverse linguistic backgrounds.

Franz's book fills a necessary gap, as it directly offers teachers direction and plans for assessing student writing. It does so by advancing an important undervalued point: Attending to the linguistic variations of all students is better and beneficial for all student writers. I want to be quite clear here in making a point about a throughline I read in Franz's instruction—that white students' writing can benefit from the influence of rhetorical patterns from other linguistic varieties. I recall here Bonnie J. Williams-Farrier's argument in her provocative essay—"'Talkin'bout Good & Bad' Pedagogies: Code-Switching vs. Comparative Rhetorical Approaches"—that the African American verbal tradition offers rhetorical resources to students from other linguistic backgrounds, and not only to African American writers. Therefore, that verbal tradition must be integrated and become fully a part of writing and rhetoric instruction.

Franz's also adeptly locates her book in the tripartite disciplines of her training, which anticipates the book's audiences: those in education, linguistics, and writing studies. Franz's discussions of teaching and assessing language bring these fields together to offer a book-length, scholarly resource guide to both pre- and in-service teachers, as well as to writing teachers taking the teacher training courses through composition camps and writing programs. I daresay that writing center training courses would also find this book wonderfully useful.

What's vitally important to me and to the reason I began this foreword with context from 2020 is that Franz unabashedly bases her discussions on her experiences and research on African American language (AAL). Her work makes me think of Rusty Barrett's observations in *Other People's English: Code Meshing, Code Switching and African American Literacy* (Young et al., 2018). Barrett says that when he conducts linguistic research across the globe in international communities, his research subjects ask him to teach them the U.S. language they most want to learn: AAL (and not so-called standard English). This comports with linguist Geneva Smitherman's recent observation that the mainstream has crossed over to us, to AAL (Alim, 2012).

Franz and teachers using this book can continue to push these boundaries even further—by showing the explicit value of Black discursive styles and AAL to language and writing instruction for all students. Here I am speaking directly to white readers, particularly white women who, statistics show, still dominate the teaching profession (at least in kindergarten to secondary school and in college writing programs). A book like Franz's helps these teachers take an autoethnographic and personal sociocultural impulse toward interrogating the ways their own white racial backgrounds and cultures impact or even impede effective writing pedagogies, and the ways that they must manage those impulses to promote academic success for all students, not just ones that match their own backgrounds. These teachers will do well to acknowledge their own and students' accents and language varieties. For as Coleman (1997) suggested in his foundational article, "Our Students Write with Accents":

> Academic English is just another language variety. Structurally, its surface features are not significantly more complex than those of other language varieties such as African American Vernacular English (AAVE). No language variety is inherently inferior or superior to another, but no language variety can be separated from the assumptions and practices which drive interactions between people. (p. 486)

The "interactions between people" include important ones between teacher and students, both in classroom instruction, writing exercises, and in assessing students' graded work. Teachers articulate this need to me when I am speaking to them across international contexts. I have begun referencing this book to speak to our colleagues who experience the same "dilemmas of interaction" but can't, won't, or don't know how to express those dilemmas or deal with them in the context of teaching, learning (their own included), and assessment. So much then goes unsaid, so much attention not paid to important possibilities for learning and sharing language. Remember, as linguist Rosina Lippi-Green reminds us in her ground-breaking book *English With an Accent* (Lippi-Green, 2012), that we must know the truth about standard language ideology and discrimination to speak truth to its power, even to our own powers. And we must resist being further stifled or lulled into standardized inertia because of our inability or not having an opportunity to name the problems of our classrooms, particularly ones we can control. Instead, we must seek knowledge and opportunity, which I daresay Franz's work here provides.

I appreciate Hannah Franz and Teachers College Press for giving me space to share some opening words about this work. It is my hope they assist in making this book one of the central texts in teaching writing for and to diverse students in the 21st century.

—Vershawn Ashanti Young

REFERENCES

Alim, H. S. (2012). Interview with Geneva Smitherman. *Journal of English Linguistics*, *40*(4), 357–377.

American Studies Association. (2020). President's statement on Black Lives Matter and the Rebellion of 2020. https://www.theasa.net/about/news-events announcements/asa-presidents-statement-black-lives-matter-rebellion-2020

Baker-Bell, A., Williams-Farrier, B. J., Jackson, D., Johnson, L., Kynard, C., & McMurtry, T. (2020). This ain't another statement! This is a DEMAND for Black linguistic justice! Conference on College Composition and Communication. https://cccc.ncte.org/cccc/demand-for-black-linguistic-justice

Coleman, C. F. (1997). Our students write with accents. Oral paradigms for ESD students. *College Composition and Communication*, *48*(4), 486–500.

Levenson, E. (2021, March 30). Former officer knelt on George Floyd for 9 minutes and 29 seconds—not the infamous 8:46. CNN. https://www.cnn.com/2021/03/29/us/george-floyd-timing-929-846/index.html

Lippi-Green, R. (2012). *English with an accent: Language ideology and discrimination in the United States* (2nd ed.). Routledge.

Mckoy, T., Shelton, C.D., Sackey, D., Jones, N. N., Haywood, C., Wourman, J-L., & Harper, K. C. (2020). CCCC Black Technical and Professional Communication Position Statement with Resource Guide, Conference on College Composition and Communication, September 2020. https://cccc.ncte.org/cccc/black-technical-professional-communication

National Council of Teachers of Mathematics. (2020). A Statement on George Floyd, Breonna Taylor, and Ahmaud Arbery. https://www.nctm.org/News-and-Calendar/News/NCTM-News-Releases/A-Statement-on-George-Floyd,-Breonna-Taylor,-and-Ahmaud-Arbery/

Silva, D. (2022). 3 officers found guilty on federal charges in George Floyd's killing. NBC News. https://www.nbcnews.com/news/us-news/jury-reaches-verdict-federal-trial-3-officers-george-floyds-killing-rcna17237

Treisman, R. (2021, April 1). Darnella Frazier, teen who filmed Floyd's murder, praised for making verdict possible. NPR. https://www.npr.org/sections/trial-over-killing-of-george-floyd/2021/04/21/989480867/darnella-frazier-teen-who-filmed-floyds-murder-praised-for-making-verdict-possib

Williams-Farrier, B. J. (2017). "Talkin' bout good and bad" pedagogies: Code-switching vs. comparative rhetorical approaches. *College Composition and Communication*, *69*(2), pp. 230–259.

Young, V. A. (2020). *This ain't yesterday's literacy: Culture and education after George Floyd*. Fountainhead Press.

Young, V. A., Balester, V., & Davies, F. (2021). Teaching writing after George Floyd. *Open Words: Access and English Studies, 13*(1), 100. https://wac.colostate.edu/docs/openwords/v13n1/youngetal.pdf

Young, V. A., Barrett, R., Rivera, Y. L., & Lovejoy, K. B. (2018). *Other people's English: Code-meshing, code-switching, and African American literacy*. Parlor Press.

- Rewards linguistic flexibility rather than linguistic assimilation so that students can develop as individual writers and make decisions about their language in their writing (Chapters 3, 4, 5, and 6)
- Validates and fosters the language of Black students for its rhetorical power and cultural and community meaning (Chapters 4, 5, and 6)

THE TIME IT TAKES TO GRADE

If there is one thing all writing instructors have in common regarding grading, it may be how much time we spend doing it. When you're teaching, how much of your time goes to grading? Again, grading, for many of us who teach writing, means much more than assigning a letter or number grade (Baker, 2014). When we say we have to grade, we often mean carefully reading students' work to give extensive written, or maybe even audio or video, comments and probably aligning students' writing with a rubric or a checklist. Thus, although *grading* technically refers to summative evaluation, many of us also use the term to refer to formative feedback—feedback to help students revise and improve their writing. Some instructors separate their formative and summative feedback, whereas others use the two types of feedback together. For example, an instructor teaching a process approach might give only formative comments on a first draft and only a letter grade and completed rubric on a final draft. Another instructor might provide a single version of a student paper with both a grade and comments to help the student improve on future assignments; these comments may or may not be directly related to the grade. Regardless of your grading and feedback processes, you likely devote much time and energy to this work.

Consider the time you've put into learning to teach. This learning might have taken the form of formal classes or degrees. It might include trainings, workshops, conferences, or other professional development. Maybe you were or are a teaching assistant with the opportunity to learn from a supervising faculty member. Perhaps you've had to learn how to teach mainly on the job, learning from your own experience and conversations with colleagues. Maybe you seek out books and articles on teaching for ideas.

Now, think about how much of your learning to teach has been devoted to learning to grade. Baker (2014) describes grading and feedback as "too often treated as an individual activity [writing instructors] should already know how to do" (p. 47). While writing instructors devote a large portion of time to reading and grading student work, relatively little pedagogical training is dedicated to the practice of grading and feedback. While working on my master's degree in reading/writing/literacy, I took courses on assessment. My classmates and I read and discussed research on writing feedback. I learned about authentic assessments, portfolios, and rubrics.

My instructors intentionally modeled particular approaches to commenting on our written work. We learned about the multiple processes that go into grading. A college writing instructor whose degrees are in areas outside of literacy education would most likely not share my experience. This book allows writing instructors, and other instructors who teach writing-intensive courses, to learn more about the grading and feedback processes that take so much time and effort.

Even as this book offers the opportunity to learn more about grading, I have written it for busy instructors. I understand the day-to-day reality of many writing instructors means both time and programmatic constraints on what you can teach and how you can assess what you teach. And extensive teaching loads can prohibit writing instructors from providing the meaningful feedback they wish to give (M. Lee, 2009). Thus, while I summarize some necessary background in this first chapter, the following chapters center on practical recommendations that consider the daily realities of writing instruction. These recommendations can apply to both formative feedback and summative evaluation. Chapters 2 through 6 each end with a list of grading and feedback practices that writing instructors can implement immediately to support effective and inclusive grading.

WHAT MOTIVATED ME TO WRITE THIS BOOK

My vision for socially and linguistically just education motivated me to write this book. This vision stems from my experiences as a student in Richmond, Virginia, public schools; an undergraduate linguistics major; a reading teacher in Norfolk, Virginia, public schools; and a teaching assistant and writing instructor in racially and linguistically diverse four-year and community college settings. As a white teacher within these settings, I continually strive to be a "dreamkeeper" for African American students by "questioning (and preparing [my] students to question) the structural inequality, the racism, and the injustice" of educational systems (Ladson-Billings, 2009, p. 140). This purpose takes on a particular urgency at the time of writing this book, just following the Supreme Court decision that extremely limited race-based affirmative action in college admissions (*Students for Fair Admissions v. Harvard,* 2023).

As a linguistics major, I was curious about variations in responses to my writing from different professors, especially across disciplines. I was also perplexed because some professors graded linguistic features such as organization, word choice, and grammar even though they did not discuss them in class. Later, in my sociolinguistics master's program, my fellow student Ashley Burns and I conducted a case study of first-year composition and writing center practices at a large research university (Burns & Franz, 2009). We learned that, while instructors referred students to the writing center for grammar help, the writing center did not aim to provide grammar support or train their tutors in grammar instruction. It seemed that students were being graded on grammar, yet no one was teaching them how to be successful in this area. As a student of English language variation—in both undergraduate and graduate school—I was concerned about how the writing assessment practices I experienced and observed impacted students whose language encompassed Black language practices and African American English. *Black language practices* is "a general term for people's language use that emphasizes a connection to the broader Black diaspora," and *African American English* is "a language variety predominantly used by African Americans and in places where African Americans live" (Charity Hudley et al., 2022, p. 3). These are the terms and definitions I adopt throughout the book, although as Charity Hudley and colleagues (2022) go on to explain, no term "can perfectly capture the richness and complexity of the Black linguistic experience in the United States" (p. 2).

While pursuing my doctorate, I worked with the William & Mary Scholars Undergraduate Research Experience (WMSURE), an undergraduate research program for students from backgrounds underrepresented at the College of William & Mary. I learned that undergraduate research was a high-impact educational practice that contributed to students thriving in college and is particularly impactful for underrepresented students (Kuh, 2008; Lopatto, 2007). The WMSURE directors and I coauthored a book for college students to guide them in making the most out of college through undergraduate research (Charity Hudley et al., 2017). Our book helps students take full advantage of the university setting's academic resources and addresses the challenges that high-achieving, underrepresented students face.

During my time with WMSURE, I also gained experience working with students in writing-intensive courses, another high-impact educational practice (Kuh, 2008). I saw the impacts of different approaches to writing feedback on high-achieving Black college students. From my mentor, Dr. Anne Charity Hudley, I learned to draw on my literacy education background to provide writing feedback that fostered students' critical thinking about their content, audience, and communication strategies. This type of feedback ensured that a writing-intensive course did, indeed, serve as a high-impact practice for our students.

I listened to WMSURE students share their experiences with professors who provided different types of writing feedback. On the one hand, some professors questioned students' preparedness for college writing and exhibited low expectations for Black student writers, especially first-generation Black college students. On the other hand, there were professors with high expectations for all students who failed to convey the specifics of such expectations, leaving students to guess how to get good grades on class papers. I knew such guessing games had the potential to disproportionately impact speakers of Black language practices and students whose high school experiences excluded them from college preparatory writing (Delpit, 2006). Moreover, low and unstated expectations would likely mitigate the positive impacts of writing-intensive courses for Black students. To learn more, I systematically studied feedback and grades on college writing. I use the findings of this study to provide analysis and recommendations for writing instructors throughout this book. The Supreme Court decision on affirmative action (*Students for Fair Admission v. Harvard,* 2023) further compels this work, as grading itself can play a role in affirmative action. When we grade, we provide or deny opportunities, and when these grades stem from a student's language patterns or prior education, we often structure such opportunities around racial lines.

SOCIOLINGUISTIC CONCEPTS THAT INFORM THIS BOOK

Key sociolinguistic concepts inform this book's recommendations for grading and feedback. Based on sociolinguistic evidence, language varies, and all languages and language varieties are equal linguistically (Lippi-Green, 2012). Language varies due to internal linguistic pressures, external social influences, and creative expression (Lippi-Green, 2012). Although knowledge of language variation is often rooted in spoken language, sociolinguists and education scholars have also documented social variation in written language (A. Banks, 2005; Grieve, 2016). Moreover, students draw on spoken language variation in their class writing in composition courses, often purposefully (Gilyard & Richardson, 2001; Hankerson, 2017; Perryman-Clark, 2012, 2013a; Smitherman, 1994). For example, students use African American English grammar and phonological patterns to define an idea or cultural concept, discuss and exemplify code-switching, and distinguish rhetorical situations (Perryman-Clark, 2013a). The Conference on College Composition and Communication (CCCC, 1974) has a longstanding resolution, *Students' Right to Their Own Language,* stating that all language varieties are equal and that educators must "respect diversity and uphold the rights of students to their own language" (para 1).

Yet, grading writing tends to make the opposite assumption: that a particular language variety is superior (Inoue, 2015; Lippi-Green, 2012). This variety may be called academic, edited, or standard English. Taking my cue from sociolinguists who work in education (e.g., Charity Hudley & Mallinson, 2011, 2014), I prefer to call the variety standardized English to highlight the processes that create and recreate language standards. Grading is one of these processes. Grading works against language variation when it aims to standardize writing as much as possible (Lippi-Green, 2012). This approach can fail student papers because of Black language practices.

Despite the role of grading in standardization, many educators seek to honor students' right to their own language, teach students to make rhetorical linguistic choices, *and* teach students dominant writing conventions (Charity Hudley & Mallinson, 2014; Delpit, 2012; Villanueva, 2001). Yet, instructors often prioritize dominant conventions to the detriment of the other two goals (Ball & Lardner, 2005; Gere et al., 2015; Royster, 2002). My research findings demonstrated that feedback that responds to student language use often rewards dominant conventions only, even when instructors have other goals. When grading does not penalize language variation, instructor comments still may value dominant conventions over language variation. This approach assigns good grades on papers, but counter to a linguistically inclusive approach, it is despite the use of Black language practices.

Assuming the linguistic equality of all languages and language varieties, sociolinguists question standard language ideologies that privilege and neutralize the language of particular, mainly white and middle-class speakers (Charity Hudley, 2017; Lippi-Green, 2012). These standard language ideologies prevent educational opportunities for students with diverse language backgrounds, who must learn to assimilate linguistically for academic success, whereas more standardized language speakers do not have to know other language varieties to be successful in school (Baker-Bell, 2017; Charity Hudley & Mallinson, 2011; Lippi-Green, 2012).

Sociolinguistics has historically associated language and race in reductive ways (Charity Hudley, 2017). To counter these associations, the study of language and race through raciolinguistics views racial identity and language variety as fluid rather than fixed categories (Alim, 2016; Blake, 2016). Blake (2016) illustrates this fluidity through a raciolinguistic analysis of her earlier study of language variation among second-generation Caribbean American and African American New Yorkers—a study that found similarities and differences in speakers' pronunciation. Blake explains, "Black New Yorkers are using linguistic resources available to them to do identity work on multiple levels . . . African American/Black people will continue to reinvent themselves and their language(s)" (pp. 164–165). A linguistically inclusive grading approach assumes that students similarly use their evolving linguistic resources to express their identity. Moreover, instructors working in a linguistically inclusive grading approach can support students in adding to their available linguistic resources and cultivating a writer's voice that speaks to their fluid identities.

While sociolinguistics continues to work toward more complex interpretations of race and language (Charity Hudley & Mallinson, 2019), the field also has the potential for research that creates equitable educational opportunities concerning language and race (Charity Hudley, 2017; Paris, 2012). Part of this potential stems from the detailed descriptions that sociolinguistics can offer—descriptions that researchers can, in turn, develop into practical advice for educators (Charity Hudley, 2017). A linguistically inclusive approach to grading thus uses detailed linguistic descriptions to honor students' right to their own language and teach students to make rhetorical linguistic choices in their writing. From a raciolinguistic perspective, these detailed descriptions allow instructors to explain how a particular language pattern works without necessarily labeling the pattern—thus allowing for more fluid categories. For example, rather than label a verb pattern like *have went* as nonstandard or informal, an instructor can explain the pattern:

> Here, *went* follows a regular verb pattern (*they went, they have went*). It can also follow an irregular pattern (*they went,* but *they have gone*)

At the same time, a linguistically inclusive grading approach names and acknowledges the rhetorical power of African American English. So the instructor might add something like, "The use of the regular pattern can engage your intended readers." This approach makes room to reward students because of their use of Black language practices, including African American English.

This book's recommendations also draw on the sociolinguistic principle of audience design (Bell, 1984). According to audience design, individuals shift their linguistic style based on direct and indirect audiences (Bell, 1984). Writing curricula often explicate goals for teaching students to vary their writing according to their audience. Many Black student writers are adept at this skill, using standardized English patterns in their writing but also employing Black language rhetorical patterns to reach or refer to a particular audience (Ball, 1996; Gilyard & Richardson, 2001; Kynard, 2007; Perryman Clark, 2012, 2013a). Yet, writing classrooms tend to prioritize teaching students to write to explicitly academic and implicitly white audiences as instructors are compelled by time constraints and classrooms of students with varying levels of experience in dominant writing conventions. Even within these constraints, a linguistically inclusive approach helps instructors draw on the rhetorical skills that many Black student writers develop based on their need to reach different audiences across race and language variety. Importantly, linguistically inclusive feedback asks students, "Who are you writing for and to?" (Giovanni, 2007).

THE BENEFITS OF A LINGUISTICALLY INCLUSIVE APPROACH TO GRADING

A linguistically inclusive approach to grading honors students' right to their own language and Black linguistic justice. We want to support college students' rich, skillful writing that engages multiple audiences. Language variation is necessary to this goal. When it comes to Black language practices, our students can work toward writing that "centers the cultural beauty—or aesthetic—in Black literature" (McMurty, 2023, p. 75). Muiru (2021) and Chapter 3 of this volume list literature that employs Black aesthetics. Many of these examples are young adult literature, works that highly engage many students who may be uninspired by other genres. Our students likewise want to write compellingly. Therefore, a linguistically inclusive approach to grading rewards, rather than penalizes, students' use of their own language and voice, including Black language.

This approach upholds the critical principles of *Students' Right to Their Own Language* (CCCC, 1974) and the more recent CCCC position, *This Ain't Another Statement! This is a DEMAND for Black Linguistic Justice!* (Baker-Bell et al., 2020). The demands in Baker-Bell and colleagues (2020) include that "teachers stop policing Black students' language practices and penalizing them for using it in the classroom" and "teachers stop promoting and privileging White Mainstream English, code-switching, and contrastive analysis at the expense of Black Language speakers" (para. 12). The chapters that follow demonstrate, with specific examples, how instructors can adopt a linguistically inclusive approach to grading to "acknowledge and celebrate Black students' use of Black Language in all its linguistic and cultural glory" (Baker-Bell et al., 2020, para. 10), as well as preserve student meaning. And the same can be true of a linguistically inclusive approach for any of your students' language varieties beyond standardized English. In these ways, a linguistically inclusive grading approach avoids racial and linguistic bias and uses culturally sustaining feedback (Paris, 2012).

A linguistically inclusive approach to grading can help students make rhetorical linguistic choices. Many writing courses aim to teach students to make rhetorical choices, especially concerning audience and purpose, when they write. Writing in different forms for different audiences is part of what makes writing-intensive courses a high-impact educational practice (Kuh, 2008). In alignment with this objective, a linguistically inclusive approach to grading rewards linguistic flexibility for multiple audiences rather than linguistic assimilation for a homogenous audience. Accordingly, comments in this approach convey value for critical thinking over compliance. Such a model of linguistic agency is necessary for guiding learners to be successful not only as students but also as independent scholars prepared to excel in college (Charity Hudley et al., 2017; Looker, 2016).

The following chapters exemplify feedback that values rhetorical choices and multiple audiences and contrasts that feedback with feedback that values compliance and one audience type. While instructors seek to teach both dominant conventions and rhetorical linguistic choices, writing feedback often favors the former. A linguistically inclusive approach can help you also reward rhetorical linguistic choices and writing for various audiences. As college students use large-language-model generative artificial intelligence (AI), like Chat GPT (Open AI, 2023), to assist with their writing in an increasing variety of ways (Terry, 2023), teaching critical thinking about rhetorical choices and voice may become even more important for instructors.

A linguistically inclusive approach to grading can facilitate students' use of feedback. Reviews of studies on feedback and learning show that effective feedback is specific, supportive, and nonevaluative (Shute, 2008). Effective feedback is vital for any writing course, and especially in online classes where instructor–student interactions may be more restricted. In a linguistically inclusive approach, feedback follows these best practices with specific linguistic descriptions rather than evaluations. Critical feedback may motivate Black college students most when instructors refer to high standards they believe the student can meet (Cohen et al., 1999; see Chapter 3). A linguistically inclusive approach attends to these higher standards by describing language variation and Black language practices as strengths and pushing students to think rhetorically about their language.

Instructors using a linguistically inclusive grading approach make comments that provide specific descriptions and ask students strategic questions about language patterns (see Chapter 4). These feedback types have been particularly effective in supporting African American student writers (Alston, 2012). Specific descriptions and strategic questions can encourage all students to think critically while they revise, understanding their options for revision or future papers. In contrast, feedback in the form of corrections can obscure the "why" of revision, and feedback in the form of labeling (e.g., "confusing sentence structure") can obscure the "how" of revision. A linguistically inclusive grading approach draws students' attention to the why and how of revising language use in writing. For instructors who do not use a process approach and instead grade and comment on single versions of student papers, this benefit can apply to comments designed to encourage improvement on future assignments.

Standardized English tends to be defined by what it is not rather than what it is (Lippi-Green, 2012). When used in feedback, such descriptions can leave students unsure of what their corrected papers should look like. Instead, a linguistically inclusive approach can help students understand how to apply their instructor's feedback by incorporating specific descriptions of language patterns (see Chapter 4). A linguistically inclusive approach can also build students' awareness of language variation and language standardization processes.

IS A LINGUISTICALLY INCLUSIVE GRADING APPROACH FOR ME?

Is a linguistically inclusive grading approach for me if departmental policies limit my grading methods? Yes! A wide range of curricular objectives and grading schemes can be implemented with a linguistically inclusive interpretation. The following chapters will discuss common curricular goals for rhetorical knowledge, conventions, and critical thinking through a linguistically inclusive lens. Although value for variation is a crucial concept underlying a linguistically inclusive approach, there are strategies throughout the book that instructors can implement even when they are expected to teach and grade on a single type of writing. And if a singular emphasis on standardized English is framed as in the student's best interest, it's important to consider whether that focus is indeed benefiting students. As Baker-Bell's (2017) students point out, in the long run, only using standardized English often isn't to their benefit: Many students will be discriminated against, even as writers, regardless of whether they are using standardized English; and many successful writers create compelling works using language variation beyond standardized English (see also Young et al., 2018).

As you go through the rest of the book, I encourage you to take a broad view of the concepts and strategies discussed, allowing yourself to adopt what you can, given your program constraints. Many of the chapters end with lists of recommended practices. Start with what works for you. The last chapter provides more examples of how to make necessary adaptations.

Is a linguistically inclusive approach for me if I use contract grading? In contract grading, a contract between the instructor and students establishes criteria for earning a particular final grade. The contract frees up the instructor to emphasize formative feedback—qualitative comments to foster students' writing development rather than to explain a grade—on individual papers. Most of the examples throughout the book apply to formative comments. Even when I discuss grading criteria, the principles I recommend can be used for the criteria in a grading contract. A linguistically inclusive approach to contract grading will focus contract criteria on rhetorical variation and the strengths of Black language practices. As such, the approach meets common contract grading goals for antiracist grading that eschews linguistic assimilation (see Inoue, 2015).

Is a linguistically inclusive approach for me if I teach mostly high-achieving students? Is this approach needed for my high-achieving students? Absolutely. There is a fundamental imperative for a linguistically inclusive grading approach for many high-achieving Black students and students from underrepresented backgrounds. The technical application of expected writing conventions may be easy for such students. Yet, many high-achieving Black students, as well as other students, are making acute sacrifices to apply these conventions—sacrifices of their voice, their language, and even who they are (Young et al., 2018). As writing instructors, we may not see students making these sacrifices but only see the result of an A paper. In a linguistically inclusive grading approach, students can be successful in their writing class without making such sacrifices. This approach also provides feedback that supports students' writing development within their own voice.

Is a linguistically inclusive grading approach for me if I teach online classes? Because a linguistically inclusive approach facilitates student engagement with feedback, it can be advantageous in online classes. Especially in online asynchronous classes, where student–instructor interactions may be limited, instructors can capitalize on feedback as a conversation and an important teaching tool. A linguistically inclusive grading approach aims for feedback as conversation in any context, and if you teach online, you might pay special attention to how to enact this use of feedback in your classes.

Is a linguistically inclusive grading approach for me if my students use language patterns beyond African American English? As you consider the descriptions of language patterns throughout this book, you can keep in mind that language is evolving and language varieties are fluid. Many of this book's examples are patterns common in African American English and may also be found in language practices used by white speakers in the southern United States. African American English and African American and Black identity are salient to the students quoted or whose writing is featured in the book. Throughout the book, I additionally refer to language patterns, such as variation in sentence structure and essay introductions, that students might use to make their writing more or less conversational in ways that cross English language varieties.

Your students likely use a range of language patterns, which may include Black language practices beyond African American English, that may or may not overlap with those I have exemplified. So, college students who are first- or second-generation immigrants from the Caribbean or Africa may use language patterns that cross the Black diaspora and patterns—including in pronunciation, vocabulary, spelling, and punctuation—that are tied to their more specific identities within the diaspora (Blake, 2016; Smith, 2019). Like African American students and faculty, Black Caribbean and African students and faculty face linguistic racism and discrimination; such discrimination often includes misrepresenting Black Caribbean students as non-native English speakers (Smith, 2019).

A linguistically inclusive grading approach can counteract this linguistic discrimination for students who use any language variety. As a few examples, Chapter 2 recommends examining the language patterns of your students, Chapter 3 recommends reading for student meaning, and Chapter 4 recommends rethinking labels and using strategic questions and specific description instead. These practices can help instructors learn about any of their students' language varieties with an open mind, regardless of what such language varieties are.

Why does a linguistically inclusive approach matter when students use generative AI to help write their papers? Students and other writers can use large-language-model generative AI, like ChatGPT (OpenAI, 2023), for writing tasks such as applying standardized mechanical and grammatical conventions, outlining a paper, generating facts and ideas, or writing in a specified style (Bishop, 2023; Learn Prompting, 2023; Terry, 2023). Generative AI is often most effective with writing tasks when user prompts name part of the rhetorical context—who the writer is, who the audience is, or what the purpose is (Learn Prompting, 2023). These are the factors that we want students to base their writing decisions on and the factors emphasized in a linguistically inclusive approach. Students have to understand these factors to effectively prompt generative AI. They also need to learn how to evaluate the writing and language that AI generates for them before applying them to their own work. A linguistically inclusive approach to feedback can guide students to work with generative AI critically and effectively.

Generative AI uses the same language patterns as the large language models on which they have been trained, which bias toward standardized English. Meanwhile, a linguistically inclusive approach values linguistic agency over linguistic assimilation. Generative AI must often be strategically primed to go beyond traditional writing patterns or to use language varieties such as African American English. If we want students to write in their own language and voice, their generative AI prompts must use explicit description of language patterns, audience, and the writer's intended style (Learn Prompting, 2023)—all of which are hallmarks of linguistically inclusive feedback. Generative AI can even imitate a writer's voice (Bishop, 2023). But, to prompt it to do so, a student writer must decide what they want their voice to sound like in a given context so they can provide the tool with examples. Linguistically inclusive grading helps students make these decisions and even make better use of generative AI.

MULTICULTURAL EDUCATION AND CULTURALLY SUSTAINING PEDAGOGY

A linguistically inclusive grading approach is guided by multicultural education theories and their application to higher education for Black students (Banks, 2020; Charity Hudley et al., 2022). Banks (2020) identifies five dimensions of multicultural education: equity pedagogy, content integration, knowledge construction, prejudice reduction, and empowering school culture. While Banks constructed this model primarily for P–12 practitioners, recent scholarship applies Banks's work to higher education (Charity Hudley et al., 2022). Charity Hudley and colleagues and Calhoun and colleagues (2021) critically document multicultural education practices that enact justice for Black college students in linguistics. I similarly use Banks's model in this book to advance educational justice in college writing classrooms. Banks's dimensions of multicultural education underlie a linguistically inclusive grading approach in the following ways:

Equity pedagogy. Equity pedagogy is a primary goal of a linguistically inclusive grading approach. In an equity pedagogy, writing instructors adapt their grading and feedback practices "in ways that will facilitate the academic achievement of students from diverse groups" (Banks, 2020, p. 18), including speakers of African American English and other language varieties. To facilitate such academic achievement, a linguistically inclusive approach to grading rewards linguistic flexibility rather than linguistic assimilation.

Content integration. In this book, content integration is about how writing assessment incorporates students' language and identities (Muhammad, 2020). Banks describes the contributions approach, the additive approach, the transformation approach, and the social action approach to content integration. In a multicultural education model, Banks recommends the transformation and social action approaches. For grading and responding to language variation in student writing, these approaches take the following forms:

- **Contributions approach:** In this approach, a writing course may have one or two special, usually informal, assignments where instructors allow language varieties such as African American English. African American English is corrected, penalized, or labeled informal in other assignments.
- **Additive approach:** Instructors reward uses of African American English or nonstandardized English they see as intentional. Instructors penalize or correct, using a code-switching model, African American English patterns that they conclude are unintentional. The instructor determines whether African American English is appropriate or inappropriate and labels language patterns as such.
- **Transformation approach:** Instructors encourage and support students' written language variation, including African American English, rather than "allow" African American English or other language varieties in specified contexts (Kynard, 2007, p. 342). In a transformation approach, instructors do not penalize language varieties such as African American English in writing assignments; instead, feedback indicates the positive functions of African American English patterns in student writing.
- **Social action approach:** Instructors reward African American English and student linguistic agency. Instructor feedback indicates the positive functions of African American English, equips students to make rhetorical linguistic decisions, and points students to venues for reaching an audience beyond the classroom.

Throughout the following chapters, I recommend practices so that instructors can assess language variation and African American English in student writing within the transformation and social action approaches. The contributions and additive approaches are more common in traditional writing pedagogy that does not use linguistically inclusive grading.

Knowledge construction. In a linguistically inclusive grading approach, instructors do not assume a standard language ideology—that is, that standardized English is superior (Lippi-Green, 2012). Instead, instructors respond to papers with questions to help students understand how writing standards are constructed and reconstructed.

Prejudice reduction. A linguistically inclusive grading approach reduces prejudicial responses to students' written language. Instructors do not penalize written African American English or use labels such as *inappropriate*, *confusing*, *incorrect*, or *informal*. Instead, instructors provide descriptive comments that tie students' language use to their purpose and multiple audiences (see Chapter 4).

Empowering school culture. An empowering school culture addresses grouping practices at institutional and programmatic levels. Although this book focuses on the classroom level, writing program administrators can scale up recommended methods, applying principles of a linguistically inclusive grading approach to writing course placement and program-level pass rates for a program that empowers African American students.

In addition to Banks's model of multicultural education, a linguistically inclusive grading approach is grounded in the established K–12 principles of culturally relevant (Ladson-Billings, 2009) and culturally sustaining pedagogies (Alim & Paris, 2017). Other models for higher education (Charity Hudley et al., 2022) also draw on culturally relevant and sustaining pedagogies. Ladson-Billings defines culturally relevant pedagogy as "the antithesis of assimilationist teaching" (p. 25) and describes culturally relevant teachers as coaching students toward excellence. One way that a linguistically inclusive grading approach is culturally relevant is that it can communicate to students, "Let's bring your language into this class. Use your own language to be an excellent writer." Culturally sustaining pedagogy builds on theories of cultural relevance to further "perpetuate and foster . . . linguistic, literate, and cultural pluralism" and "sees the outcome of learning as additive rather than subtractive" (Alim & Paris, 2017, p. 1). Muhammad (2020) describes a culturally sustaining pedagogy that cultivates the literacy genius of Black students. A linguistically inclusive grading approach becomes culturally sustaining when it communicates: "I support your success in this class and as a Black and African American English writer. I support you in changing the power structure of academic writing."

The examples provided throughout this book will allow instructors to adapt their current approach to provide culturally relevant and culturally sustaining feedback. While culturally sustaining writing feedback examples are infrequently documented in the literature, many college writing scholars have researched and established other writing instructional practices that are culturally sustaining for Black students. For example, Elaine Richardson,

Staci Perryman-Clark, April Baker-Bell, and Vershawn Ashanti Young and his colleagues have implemented curriculum and instruction based on the SRTOL position. Their pedagogical models validate and foster the language of Black students. An instructor who wants to implement a linguistically inclusive approach to grading does not have to revise their entire curriculum. At the same time, it is crucial to recognize how a linguistically inclusive grading approach aligns with other culturally sustaining practices for the college writing classroom.

In Afrocentric writing pedagogy, for instance, African American English is not less applicable to academic writing than standardized varieties of writing (Perryman-Clark, 2013b; Richardson, 2000). Students from different language backgrounds learn African American linguistic practices while drawing on and extending their own linguistic repertoire (Perryman-Clark, 2013b; Richardson, 2000, 2003). Richardson (2000) explains that incoming college students have been educated through either a white-centric college preparatory curriculum or a white-centric curriculum without college preparation. And students of color have been disproportionately educated in the latter. The impact of this education, or miseducation (Woodson, 1933/1990), is that African American college students have internalized negative perceptions of their own language, especially its use in the classroom and writing, as many scholars have found among their own students (Baker-Bell, 2020; Richardson, 2000; Young et al., 2018). African American students should not have to face the extra burden of this double consciousness to learn in the classroom: "If we truly want to develop Black students rather than transform them into people who act, sound, and write white, we must allow Black students to develop their Black voices as an academic convention" (Richardson, 2003, p. 138). Richardson's students found her course's situation of African American English as an academic language and an academic topic exciting and liberating.

Perryman-Clark (2013b) expanded Richardson's approach to look at the benefits of an Afrocentric writing pedagogy for white students in addition to Black students. Perryman-Clark aimed to "broaden our understanding of the appropriate contexts for writing in Ebonics" (Perryman-Clark, 2013b, p. 2). Her students wrote formal academic and informal writing assignments in African American English. Students read articles on African American English in rhetoric and composition and analyzed the linguistic choices of writers by understanding the relationship between language, race, and power. Students then reflected on their own linguistic choices in course writing assignments, including African American English rhetorical styles. Perryman-Clark (2012, 2013b) assessed students' writing according to their use of African American rhetorical strategies to support their paper content and according to the goals of the institution's writing program. For example, students' use and understanding of African American English demonstrated their writing skills for various purposes and in different forms and styles.

Afrocentric writing pedagogy does not necessarily exclude instruction about standardized English but does decenter standardized English to teach linguistic flexibility and expand notions of academic language.

Baker-Bell (2020) discusses a similar approach, antiracist Black language pedagogy, in a high school context. Baker-Bell offers models of learning experiences to "help students challenge, interrogate, unlearn, and work toward dismantling Anti-Black Linguistic Racism" (pp. 8–9). Baker-Bell's models teach students about the origins and linguistic features of Black language and foster students' critique of language, race, and power and development of linguistic agency.

Young and colleagues (2018) describe a code-meshing model for teaching writing. Code-meshing directly counters code-switching instruction that requires shifts to standardized English in ways that imply to students, "be yourself somewhere else" (Young et al., 2018, p. 33). Code-meshing pedagogy teaches students to write using more than one language variety. In a code-meshing model, learning is additive, whereas in a code-switching model, learning is subtractive. Young and colleagues use code meshing to teach students rhetorical variation, voice, and engaging writing—all of which are supported by linguistically inclusive grading.

While Richardson, Perryman-Clark, Baker-Bell, and Young and colleagues describe culturally sustaining curricula that follow SRTOL, this book exemplifies specific comments and grading practices that instructors can use to develop the skills necessary to be culturally sustaining teachers.

THE SIGNIFICANCE OF GRADES

Research on feedback on student writing tends to exclude grades since grades are less helpful for learning than formative feedback (Shute, 2008). Yet, grades represent real consequences for students, and research on grading practices can inform equity in writing pedagogy. As J. Lee (2016) explained, "If a social justice agenda for writing assessment is about creating opportunity structures and positive consequences for all students, then classroom grading is an obvious place to focus our efforts" (p. 175).

Grades indicate an instructor's or institution's values in writing, including language patterns (O'Neill, 2015; Scott & Inoue, 2015). And students understand that, regardless of what happens in the classroom, the most powerful consequences for them are, in the end, how they are evaluated (Broad, 2003; Inoue, 2015; Jeffery & Selting, 1999). Students, therefore, have a hard time believing instructors who try to persuade them that writing is not about grades (Jeffery & Selting, 1999). And for most students, grades are about figuring out what the teacher or professor wants, not developing individual writing goals, voice, or style. Many Black students sacrifice their own voices to get better grades. They might, for instance, avoid writing for their communities and about who they are and what they know. And they will likely be compelled to put aside their language patterns to do well. Learning opportunities thus become reductive rather than expansive as students' writing is reduced to sets of conventions separate from their identity and voice. In the classroom, these injustices are more challenging to see than failing grades. Without attention to the whole student, high grades can conceal the impacts of our racist grading structures. In a linguistically inclusive grading approach, however, a strong paper that receives a good grade is about linguistic agency, student voice, and language variation; Black students are not required to make sacrifices not expected of their white peers for writing success. In many institutions, writing course grades are gatekeepers—systematically keeping some students out of and letting other students into majors and other courses, often by rewarding and penalizing students based on dominant writing conventions (Fasching-Varner, 2009; Naynaha, 2016; Sonnenmoser, 2009). The first-year writing instructors faced with this gatekeeping role may or may not have had the opportunity to receive training in writing pedagogy and have rarely received training in sociolinguistics or writing assessment (Behrens, 2014; Cox, 2009; Matsuda, 2006; Myers & Kircher, 2007; Schneider, 2005). In this gatekeeping role, writing instructors often disproportionately fail students of color, keeping them from moving forward from prerequisite courses and on with the rest of the college curriculum (Coleman et al., 2016; Inoue, 2014; Poe et al., 2014). Taiyon Coleman, in Coleman and colleagues (2016), described her experience as a student with this reality:

> My well-meaning and well-intentioned white first-year composition teacher consistently told me, in her written feedback and final grade assessment of my paper assignments, that she could not understand what I was writing because it did not make any sense. Usually, I wrote about what I knew, which was being female, black, poor, urban, and being a first-time college student, away from home, attending a predominantly white college in the middle of the Midwest. . . . I stopped attending class, and I failed my composition course although some of the essays were being published in campus-wide publications. A year later, after failing first-year composition like most students within my identity intersections, I dropped out of college. It would take five years before I would develop the courage and opportunity to return, let alone take first-year writing. (p. 367)

Failing first-year composition influenced the overall trajectory of Coleman's next several years. This experience speaks to the impact of failing a writing course and the specific evaluation of her writing through grades and comments. It's notable that when Coleman wrote for an authentic audience via campus publications, her work was better received than when she wrote to be graded in a class and without other purpose. Coleman's story demonstrates that both writing grades themselves, as well as their associated responses, have real impacts on students. Coleman might have been able to succeed, and indeed thrive, in this course if her writing instructor had known the following:

- Who Coleman was writing for and to, and why
- African American English rhetorical patterns and their literary value
- The sacrifices Coleman would have had to make to be successful by the given criteria
- How grades can demotivate learning (Shute, 2008; Inoue, 2015)
- How to provide specific, supportive, and nonevaluative feedback (Shute, 2008)
- How to present critical feedback from the perspective of high standards that she believed Coleman could meet (Cohen et al., 1999)
- The role of an authentic purpose and audience for writing in contrast to class writing that often seems purposeless and readerless

A linguistically inclusive grading approach takes all of the foregoing into account.

Despite common experiences like Coleman's, writing instructors can inadvertently engage in grading practices that do not address the relationship between grades and opportunities. In a study of the shared evaluation practices of 50 instructors, including instructor interviews and observations, Broad (2003) found that when instructors considered benefits to the student in a pass/fail decision, they almost always decided to fail the student. In such cases, the instructors believed that the student would have better support if they failed and repeated a writing course rather than continue to struggle with writing in later classes (Broad, 2003). When considering the "benefit to student" (Broad, 2003, p. 108), then, the instructors did not take into account the following:

- The limits that a failing grade might put on a student's education (Coleman et al., 2016; Perryman-Clark, 2016; Sonnenmoser, 2009)
- The financial costs, including time-to-degree models
- The potential racial implications of these decisions (Fasching-Varner, 2009; Lee, 2016; Naynaha, 2016)
- The potentially demotivating impacts of failing grades on student learning (Helmbrecht, 2007; Inoue, 2015; Shute, 2008)
- The extent to which retaking a class aids student learning

In contrast, Helmbrecht (2007) provided an example of what it looks like to critically reflect on how failing grades may impact students. Helmbrecht explained that students who fail writing assignments tend to "have the most to lose by being told once again (this time in a college course) that they are poor/bad/struggling/remedial/basic writers" (p. 306).

The consequences of grades lead to a strong student focus on grades over other writing goals. Students will likely read instructor comments with this focus, even formative feedback intended to motivate revision rather than justify grades. These entrenched beliefs make it difficult for instructors who want students to think for themselves, demonstrate linguistic agency, or make creative choices in their writing. A linguistically inclusive approach to grading can help us explicitly communicate these expectations to students accustomed to correctness and formulas taking precedence.

HISTORICAL CONTEXT OF GRADING WRITING

The historical context of grading writing will demonstrate the position that writing instruction has traditionally occupied in higher education and how college writing has come to favor uniformity and exclusionary practices. The second half of the 19th century saw the development of university departments, including English departments, which often included literature and rhetoric or composition. Composition occupied a lower status in English departments, and institutions treated first-year writing courses as preparatory and remedial rather than intellectual (Rose, 1985; Russel, 2006). Due to this lower status, little progression in writing pedagogy and textbooks took place throughout the early 20th century (Connors, 1986).

The private historically Black colleges and universities (HBCUs) founded around the mid-19th century were liberal arts institutions with a curricular emphasis on English studies, including composition and critical literacies (Royster & Williams, 1999). In contrast, publicly funded HBCUs educated students in professional training, with the notable exception of Howard University, both a premier liberal arts institution and publicly funded (Royster & Williams, 1999). A study of writing assignments and curriculum at Howard in the 1920s revealed that professors assigned students to critically analyze race, racism, and exclusionary academic narratives (Zaluda, 1998). However, such assignments and curricula also called for linguistic assimilation (Zaluda, 1998).

Dominant narratives suppress the historical development of critical literacies by Howard and other HBCUs and instead associate African American students with remedial writing. Royster and Williams tie this dominant narrative in part to Shaughnessy's (1977) work in basic writing that responded to open admissions policies increasing socioeconomic and ethnic diversity at institutions such as the City University of New York (CUNY) (see also Horner, 1996). Despite over a century of HBCUs educating students in critical literacies and over a quarter-century of remedial writing education for white students, the 1960s saw strong associations between African American students and remedial writing that persist today (Royster & Williams, 1999).

College writing and academic grades have a shared history. The advent of written rather than oral examinations in the 1830s gave colleges the ability to rank students efficiently in a precursor to grading (Boyd, 1998).

Later, in the 1880s, Harvard University's five-letter grading system and its Freshman Composition course simultaneously became models for colleges across the country (Boyd, 1998; Crowley, 1998). Harvard developed Freshman Composition as a response to noted errors in student writing (Rose, 1985). Grades, meanwhile, have always had a role in using higher education for social control (Boyd, 1998; Cox, 2009; Veysey, 1965). Early ranking systems in colleges explicitly factored in students' social class (Cox, 2009; Smallwood, 1935). Later, grading systems implicitly drew on student social class by accounting for "conduct" (Smallwood, 1935, p. 24) as well as academic performance. The connections college leaders, such as Harvard's President Charles Eliot in the late 1860s, made between rankings or grades and character were rooted in social Darwinist and meritocratic-based justifications of maintaining the socioeconomic status quo, as well as in existing linguistic hierarchies from a fearful professional class (Boyd, 1998). Connections between grades and character appeared strongly in claims about college student writing, as educators frequently used terms such as "lazy" and "careless" to describe first-year writers and their writing (Boyd, 1998; Crowley, 1998; Tieje et al., 1915).

In the late 1800s and the early 1900s, grades on college writing perpetuated the status quo through a strong emphasis on formal correctness, often through punitive terms such as "delinquency" and "sanctions" (Boyd, 1998; Crowley, 1998; Rose, 1985). Contemporary exercise-filled textbooks similarly emphasized correctness. And writing instructors needed these textbooks to teach because their formal training was in literature rather than composition pedagogy (Connors, 1986; Russel, 2006). Writing-as-correctness also corresponded with early 20th-century educational psychology, which aimed for efficiency through precise educational outcomes measurement (Rose, 1985). In grading, the primacy of grammatical correctness was often so strong that a single grammatical error could result in a failing grade despite the rest of the paper; grammatical error was viewed as representing disorder and chaos (Tieje et al., 1915). As such, grades maintained a unified set of consistent standards and eliminated linguistic differences (Boyd, 1998). These approaches are the opposite of a linguistically inclusive approach. Even in the 19th century, some professors and students criticized the constant error correction. For example, Mary Augusta Jordan, a professor at Smith College from 1884 to 1921, described error correction's negative impacts on student writers and wrote about historical and interwriter language variation for popular audiences (Kates, 2001).

Although the obsession with grammatical error has lessened over time, educational policies and practices continue to simplify writing to quantifiable error correction "particularly when 'nontraditional' students flood our institutions" (Rose, 1985, pp. 345–346). Grades are still related to potential changes in socioeconomic hierarchies, which we have seen in concerns about grade inflation leading to declining standards (Boyd, 1998; Trimbur, 1996). Meanwhile, grade deflation encourages the gatekeeping of student writers, especially students of color, and opposes pedagogy that establishes high expectations and supports students throughout the writing process (Agnew, 1997). Today, writing assessment has continued to associate grammatical error with laziness and carelessness (Kynard, 2013), and grades are still rooted in meritocratic arguments that neutralize racialized linguistic and cultural hierarchies (Behm & Miller, 2012; Dixson & Rousseau Anderson, 2017; Fasching-Varner, 2009; Inoue, 2015). In contrast, a linguistically inclusive approach disassociates students' language backgrounds from errors and associates linguistic and racial diversity with excellence.

STUDY BACKDROP

I have based this book's analysis and recommendations on a content analysis of graded composition papers (Franz, 2019). I studied 121 graded papers from 10 assignments taken from three composition classes. Each class was taught by a different instructor: Angela, Stacey, and Susan (pseudonyms), whom I refer to throughout the book. The goal of my analysis was to answer the following research questions:

1. What linguistic features do writing instructors respond to in student class papers?
2. How are these linguistic features responded to?
3. How are these linguistic features penalized and rewarded, especially via grades?

My findings in response to question 1 form the basis of Chapters 5 and 6; findings in response to question 2 form the basis of Chapter 4; and findings in response to question 3 form the basis of Chapter 3.

COMPANION RESOURCES

In addition to the study of graded student papers, recommendations throughout the book stem from follow-up research that provided resources for Black college students and their writing instructors to support linguistic agency (Franz et al., 2021; Franz et al., 2022; Franz et al., in press). This work was funded by a Conference on College Composition and Communication Research Initiative Grant. Our research team of Black scholars included the following:

- Dr. Anne Charity Hudley, associate dean, Stanford University School of Education
- Dr. Michelle Grue, assistant professor, University of California Santa Barbara

- Angela Rowell, graduate student, San Francisco State University
- Sierra Johnson, undergraduate student, College of William & Mary
- Marie Tano, graduate student, Stanford University

We created the *Students' Right to Their Own Writing* website (srtow.org), with a section for students and a section for instructors, based on Dr. Charity Hudley's and my prior research. Our collaborators contributed their own research and experiences to the website's resources. Angela Rowell was the team's web designer and applied design principles to create the site's layout, navigation, infographics, and other graphics and images (see Franz et al., 2022; Franz et al., in press for a full description of our process).

Our research team conducted focus groups with faculty and students to get feedback on and improve the resources on the website (Franz et al., 2022). Faculty with a focus on Black language in education, writing studies, and linguistics participated. Both current Black college students and recent alums participated in our student focus groups. In particular, the insights gained from our student focus groups and the students on our research team have influenced this book's emphasis on Black student voices and understanding students' perspectives on the writing feedback they receive.

The *Students' Right to Their Own Writing* website (srtow.org) is a companion website to this book. There, readers can find additional practical resources, including graded papers and rubrics, to support the implementation of a linguistically inclusive grading approach.

OVERVIEW OF THE BOOK

I have written this book for college writing instructors and other instructors who teach writing-intensive classes. The practical analyses and recommendations consider the common reality of full teaching loads, which might mean three to six sections a semester with 60–100 or more students, and sometimes multiple preps. Thus, this book addresses how even the busiest writing instructors can give students linguistically inclusive grades and feedback. While writing this book, I have also kept other practical factors in mind. I know that not every writing instructor works in a department where they have autonomy over grading schemes and criteria. I therefore provide multiple strategies in every chapter; start with what is most feasible in your context.

The following chapters unpack common grading and feedback practices using the concepts described in this first chapter. Any writing instructors looking to make even minor improvements to their grading practice can use this book to benefit their students. Chapter 2 focuses on the curricular contexts supporting a linguistically inclusive approach to grading: course objectives, instructor motivations, and assignment goals. Chapters 3 and 4 take an in-depth look at grading processes and commenting, respectively, in support of a linguistically inclusive approach. Chapter 5 focuses on organizational structures, topic relationships, and word choice rooted in African American English rhetorical and narrative styles. Chapter 6 analyzes instructor responses to grammar and mechanics in light of African American English. Chapters 5 and 6 each give a sociolinguistic explanation of the language features explored, relate the features to African American English, describe common responses to these features from a sociolinguistic perspective, and provide examples for responding to these features using a linguistically inclusive approach. Chapter 7 summarizes a linguistically inclusive grading approach and what it can look like in *your* classroom—whether you teach a large number of students, teach high-achieving writers, teach online, use contract grading, or grade based on departmental policies; this chapter also revisits a linguistically inclusive grading approach in the context of generative AI.

SELF-ASSESS YOUR PRACTICES

Chapters 1–6 end with questions for you to self-assess your grading and feedback practices. Reflecting on these questions can help you determine how best to apply the book's analyses and recommendations to your teaching. You can use the following questions to take stock of how grading and other feedback function in your writing courses:

1. How much time do you spend grading and giving feedback on student papers during a semester?
2. Do you talk about grading and feedback processes with colleagues? If so, what do you discuss, and how do your processes compare?
3. Have you ever made changes to your grading and feedback processes? If so, why?
4. What are your primary purposes for giving students written feedback on their papers?
5. How would you describe the relationship between summative feedback (grades, scores, and the comments that explain these grades and scores) and formative feedback (feedback to help students revise or otherwise improve) in your approach?
6. Do students do anything with the feedback you provide on their papers? If so, what?
7. Who passes your writing classes? Why?
8. Who fails your writing classes? Why?
9. What, if anything, do you wish was different about your grading and feedback processes, students' interaction with your feedback, or who passes your classes?

CHAPTER 2

Curriculum and Instruction for a Linguistically Inclusive Grading Approach

Written language variation is a part of any writing class, whether intended by the instructor or not. In the examples in Chapter 1, Richardson, Perryman-Clark, and Baker-Bell explicitly teach about African American English in their writing classes. Even when writing instructors do not teach about African American English, many teach students about rhetorical situation, emphasizing varying writing based on audience, purpose, and genre. Other instructors teach students one specific way to write, but inevitably, students will vary in their writing styles to some extent regarding word choice, sentence structures, or paragraph structures and transitions. When instructors teach one specific way to write, that style encompasses dominant conventions for mechanics and grammar, with perhaps discipline- or genre-specific approaches to vocabulary and organization. These academic conventions exclude many written African American English patterns. This chapter is about course objectives, instructor experiences and motivations, and assignment goals that instructors can use to support a linguistically inclusive approach to grading.

COURSE OBJECTIVES IN SUPPORT OF LINGUISTICALLY INCLUSIVE GRADING

First-year writing programs often create shared course objectives for all instructors. Some of these objectives may align better with a linguistically inclusive approach than others. Even if you need to adhere to program-wide objectives, you can interpret these objectives to support a linguistically inclusive approach to grading.

Rhetorical Knowledge

Composition objectives often cover rhetorical knowledge. These objectives might refer to rhetorical knowledge, rhetorical awareness, rhetorical situation, or something similar. Variation is at the heart of these concepts. Rhetorical knowledge objectives ask students to vary their written language and content based on their assignment purpose, intended audience, and the assigned genre. For example, one objective from the composition course I studied was for students to "adapt voice, tone, and level of formality to a variety of rhetorical situations." The words *adapt* and *variety* indicate that students should have the opportunity to write differently for different assignments. To learn how to do this, students can identify the rhetorical moves writers make in different types of writing—especially in writing that they, the students, find engaging.

Expectations for organization or word choice, for instance, should not necessarily stay consistent across assignments. For example, students can practice organizing their writing such that their thesis is stated explicitly up front to suit readers who are likely scanning an essay for a particular purpose or action, like admissions or search committees. A former student of mine was required to write a brief personal narrative as part of an English teaching program application. She opened her narrative with the main point she wanted her reader to take away:

> Being the child of two immigrants to the US, education, especially English education, was something that I was forced into understanding at a young age.

This opener immediately addresses the writer's purpose to describe how her background influenced her to apply to the program. Although she needs to fill in with details and explanations, the reader knows from the start that the narrative will be about the writer's experience with English education as a child of immigrants. Meanwhile, in other rhetorical situations, students might organize their writing to open with a less explicit statement that piques the reader's curiosity and then gradually leads them to the main point. This structure can suit audiences reading primarily for interest and enjoyment. When Dr. Michelle Grue, assistant professor of creative studies at the University of California, Santa Barbara, assigned her class a literacy narrative, one of her students opened the assignment with:

> I had to find a new coping method to deal with this strange new life I was forced into. I felt like I was floating adrift in a sea of emotions and feelings for a long time. (Franz et al., 2021)

The student does not yet explain his strange new life or emotions but slowly takes the reader through his experiences. In the concluding paragraphs, he eventually reveals his thesis on the role of poetry in his well-being. Part of the student-writer's goal was to show rather than tell his main point. This style is reminiscent of African American rhetorical patterns discussed further in Chapter 5. This style also starkly contrasts with stating the thesis early and explicitly. Although both of the previous examples are from narratives, variation in audience and purpose coincided with variation in organizational styles. To learn to adapt their writing to rhetorical situations, students need the opportunity to write differently on different assignments and understand that conventions are not uniform across audiences and purposes. Writing across rhetorical situations contributes to the high educational impact of writing-intensive courses (Kuh, 2008).

Variation is likewise integral to sociolinguistics, so a linguistically inclusive approach to grading can be applied seamlessly to course objectives on rhetorical knowledge (see also Perryman-Clark, 2012). In a linguistically inclusive approach, instructor responses address and reward rhetorical variation rather than treating conventions as static across assignments. So, an instructor might describe how each of the foregoing openers suits the narrative's audience and the purpose:

- [This opener] addresses the application prompt—tying your background to your motivation to apply. Great for a scholarship committee that may only skim your essay or stop reading early on.
- [This opener] draws me in. I'm curious to know more about your emotions. I don't yet know where you're going, but I want to find out!

These comments describe the rhetorical moves students are making so that they can not only be rewarded for their intentional choices but also learn to be more aware of these choices to begin with.

Suppose an instructor believes a student's choice does not suit the rhetorical situation. In that case, it's essential to address the rhetorical nature of this decision instead of implying that conventions stay the same across all writing or even all college assignments:

> [This opener] catches my interest, but I don't yet know what your point is. In an application, state your purpose up front. Your reader may stop reading after the first sentence. The opener you have would suit an audience reading for interest, but your reader may want to weed out applications as quickly as possible.

Variations in more micro-level features, such as grammar and mechanics, can also be treated as rhetorical, in line with rhetorical knowledge objectives (Perryman-Clark, 2012). In an analysis of writing rubrics, Balester (2012) includes an example from a rubric from Saint Mary's University of Minnesota (2008): "Handling of grammar and mechanics enhances the reader's understanding of the writer's purpose." Here, the writer may make decisions about grammar and mechanics based on their purpose. A former student I worked with wrote a paper on the linguistic style-shifting of U.S. presidential candidates in the 2000 and 2008 elections. She used the African American English possessive form, "Obama style." The standardized form would be "Obama's style." Her use of this African American English form aligned with her purpose to describe the power of Obama's shifting between African American

English and standardized English. A linguistically inclusive grading approach rewards this rhetorical variation. Balester contrasts the rhetorical treatment of grammar and mechanics with rubrics that frame grammar as error correction for conformity with criteria such as "precise syntax" and "free of spelling, capitalization, and usage errors" (*Writer's Choice*, 2008). Through the terms *precise* and *errors*, these rubric descriptors imply that grammar and mechanics are the same regardless of the rhetorical situation. Wording like this is not in line with a linguistically inclusive approach to grading.

Conventions and Appropriateness

While rhetorical knowledge objectives can emphasize adaptation and variation, they can also direct students toward a set of conventions, such as the following:

- Use conventions of format, structure, design, and documentation appropriate to the rhetorical situation
- Edit writing with consideration to surface features, such as syntax, usage, punctuation, and spelling, that are appropriate for the rhetorical situation

A linguistically inclusive approach to these objectives assumes that conventions change. Moreover, a linguistically inclusive approach considers *who* determines what language patterns are appropriate in a particular rhetorical situation and recognizes that writers, including writing instructors and their students, can change conventions. In this approach, the student-writer determines what patterns are appropriate based on their audience, purpose, topic, genre, and their own voice and agency (Balester, 2012). The student may learn the current conventions of an assigned genre. Yet, they may also learn to veer away from those conventions in light of other aspects of their rhetorical situation, such as maintaining their voice or engaging with their audience through the use of an African American English rhetorical style.

Perryman-Clark (2012) reframes appropriateness in this way. She describes the writing of her student, Marquise, who uses African American English patterns to achieve the purpose of his writing assignments. Marquise uses a feature called field dependency (see also Gilyard & Richardson, 2001 and Chapter 5 of this volume), which uses first person to "develop analyses in relationship to others" (Perryman-Clark, 2012, p. 263). Specifically, Marquise uses the first person to identify with his claims and evidence when writing about African American rhetoric: "This takes me back to an observation I made . . ." and "We must not rule out the general purpose of writing" (p. 263).

In contrast, in a traditional approach, appropriateness might be determined in a more limited way, solely by the instructor and outside authority, such as a style manual or grammar handbook. This perspective views conventions as static and nonnegotiable, counter to a linguistically inclusive approach. In this case, the rhetorical situation may exclude the writer's voice and agency. Someone else decides what is appropriate, and the student writer conforms to those expectations. Often, African American English is counted as inappropriate in this approach. Students, in this case, may work with a reduced set of rhetorical situations, such as general academic audiences and genres, rather than the "variety of rhetorical situations" referred to in other objectives.

Composition course objectives commonly refer to appropriateness (Barbier, 2003). If your course objectives refer to appropriateness, how do you interpret it? Do students have the opportunity to determine what is appropriate based on multiple aspects of a rhetorical situation? Does the student's voice have a role in what's appropriate for the rhetorical situation? Course objectives with room for student agency, voice, and dynamic conventions can lay a foundation for a linguistically inclusive grading approach.

Critical Thinking

Critical thinking is another common composition objective. Instructors with a background in education may recognize Bloom's taxonomy of critical thinking skills following the hierarchy:

1. Remembering
2. Understanding
3. Applying
4. Analyzing
5. Evaluating
6. Creating (Bloom et al., 1956; Anderson & Krathwohl, 2001)

For example, Susan, a study participant, moves her students beyond writing that summarizes to writing that analyzes and evaluates (Franz, 2019). In a linguistically inclusive grading approach, instructors encourage students to think critically not only about their writing content and purposes but also the specific linguistic features they use.

Stacey illustrates critical thinking about linguistic features when she teaches pronoun choice (Franz, 2019). She finds that many of her students have been taught to avoid the first person in their writing. In the *apply* level of Bloom's taxonomy, students might use this convention in their writing. Stacey has students move to *analyze* by engaging with the rationale for this convention in particular genres (e.g., it is challenging to validate arguments in first person in research writing). She then teaches students how variation in pronouns can be a matter of style or purpose. Students can *evaluate* their pronoun options at this stage to *create* a style that suits their purpose, audience, and voice.

In a linguistically inclusive grading approach, responses to student writing likewise encourage students to analyze, evaluate, and even create, rather than simply apply, conventions, as in the following:

- Does your use of *you* help bring your audience into your writing or include them in your purpose? Or, does *you* here refer to someone other than the audience; if so, who? Answering these questions can help you determine how to make use of *you* in your writing.
- What is the potential impact of capitalizing this phrase versus using lowercase? What do other writers do and why? What message, if any, do you want to send about this phrase?

In contrast, simply correcting second-person pronouns or capitalization might lead students to apply writing conventions but prevent them from moving into higher-level critical thinking skills.

INSTRUCTOR MOTIVATIONS AND LINGUISTICALLY INCLUSIVE GRADING

Even when working with shared objectives, individual instructor motivations and philosophies shape writing instruction. Writing instructors may have specific beliefs about writing, education, and their students that lead to specific goals they would like their students to achieve. Often, writing instructors are motivated to do what they believe is best for their students, which may be to prepare them for future writing, push them to work to their full potential, or put all students on an equal playing field. These and similar motivations can underlie a linguistically inclusive approach, which centers on student experience and agency.

Preparing Students for Academic and Real-World Writing

First-year writing instructors may fluctuate between preparing their students primarily for academic writing and primarily for writing outside of the academy—"real-world writing," as study participant Angela put it (Franz, 2019). The instructor's focus may be influenced by their own writing practice—what genres they write, for whom, and why. To support a linguistically inclusive grading approach, instructors can keep in mind the realities of the range of writing that their students might encounter after their class. This range of writing can cover the short-term—the classes students will take next semester—to the long-term—the skills students need to adapt to new writing situations in their future professions.

From a sociolinguistic perspective, instructors need to learn the specifics of the writing students might engage in in the future. Based on research in education and cognitive psychology, it is also necessary to provide students with the metacognitive skills to adapt to new writing situations (Ambrose et al., 2010; National Research Council, 2000). You might think about other courses at your institution as your students' future writing tasks. For example, Stacey prepares her students first and foremost for their next required writing class in the sequence. Stacey is familiar with the objectives and assignments for this second course, which teaches research and argument. She scaffolds these required skills for her students, gradually assigning more outside sources for each major paper throughout the semester. Stacey is motivated by her knowledge of a more advanced course to offer students particular preparation.

First-year writing instructors also aim to prepare students for writing in their majors or other disciplines outside of composition. Rather than relying on your assumptions of what students write in different classes, you can gather current information about what students are writing at your institution. For example, you might ask your former students the following:

- What types of writing are you assigned?
- What is the purpose of these writing assignments?
- Who are the intended audiences for these writing assignments?
- Do you turn in only a final product or stages of the writing process (e.g., proposal, annotated bibliography, outline, draft)?
- What are the primary grading criteria for these assignments? How do you get an A?
- Is word choice or grammar part of the grading criteria? If so, are you taught these topics or expected to already know how to meet these criteria?

You can also reframe these questions to ask them to colleagues who teach in other departments. Answers to these questions will help you gain some sociolinguistic details about the writing expected of your students in other classes.

Real-world writing preparation motivates some writing instructors more than college writing preparation. Indeed, employers continue to value the writing skills of college graduates as potential employees (Finley, 2021). And writing to a specified audience for a specified purpose at work often feels more purposeful than writing to a vague or instructor audience to be graded in college courses. When preparing students for real-world writing, instructors might consider the common industries that college graduates work in. The five most common job groups for Black college graduates in 2014 were office and administrative support; education, training, and library; management; business and financial operations; and healthcare practitioners and technicians (NCES, 2016). These job groups stayed consistent for all college graduates, except for office and administrative support, which ranked number five for all college graduates versus number one for Black college graduates. In many of these roles, employees chiefly write status reports or updates and email or other written communication with colleagues or clients. For each of these types of writing, writers need to begin by identifying their purpose and audience. Instructors can draw attention to this fact, explaining that purpose and audience influence every type of writing. In her class, Stacey has students examine the language of emails and text messages based on audience and purpose.

At the same time, it's essential to recognize that jobs continue to evolve. We must prepare students to adapt to writing tasks that we might not readily foresee in their careers, especially with the rapid increase in the capabilities and availability of generative AI and other new technology and media. We want students to be prepared to take on new writing tasks and use new technology for these tasks critically and effectively. Following the writing experiences of college graduates, Alexander and colleagues (2020) give the example of Miguel, a Latino alum with a creative writing degree who writes advertising copy, stand-up comedy, and podcast scripts. The authors explain that although Miguel did not practice these genres in his college courses, he felt that his creative writing degree prepared him for this work. What understandings and skills can you equip your students with so that they, like Miguel, can adapt to new writing situations in their careers? A linguistically inclusive approach aligns with this perspective. In a linguistically inclusive grading approach, feedback encourages students to develop metacognitive skills, such as by asking questions that move students to the higher levels of Bloom's taxonomy. Such feedback has students consider different factors when making choices about their writing. In contrast, treating writing conventions and processes as stable across situations might not prepare students to adapt to various writing purposes, audiences, and technologies.

Angela, who wants her students to see writing as something outside of college, directs students to write for nonacademic audiences (Franz, 2019). She teaches her students journalistic attribution and MLA citation style. In a linguistically inclusive grading approach, these variations in audience and style are accompanied by strategic questions to encourage students to make decisions. For example, Angela might ask questions such as the following:

- What is your primary purpose in citing sources?
- What attribution style will be most familiar to your audience?
- How might journalistic attribution facilitate reading for your audience?
- How might MLA citation style facilitate reading for your audience?

Because feedback in this approach emphasizes variation and rhetorical decisions, students can gain skills in how to write a certain way and *how to figure out how to write* in new ways. These questions draw attention to students' metacognition—how and why they make decisions about their writing. Such feedback can set students up to consider their written work in light of their audience and purpose in the future.

Addressing Unequal Writing Preparation

First-year writing instructors often have firsthand experience with the different writing experiences of their incoming students. Because sociolinguistics examines language in context, an instructor working with a linguistically inclusive approach must understand that systemic issues, including institutional racism in K–12 education, lead to unequal writing preparation.

Some instructors find that they need to put aside their assumptions about students' prior writing experiences and instead incorporate fundamental understandings students need for the class into their teaching (Franz, 2016). One writing instructor tells students on the first day of her course, "I don't want your intelligence to be insulted, but we're going to go over some very basic things, as well as some of the harder things." The instructor is careful to use both the terms *review* and *introduce* because what she discusses will be familiar to some students yet new to others. To simultaneously draw on and build students' background knowledge, the instructor asks questions such as, "What are the basic components of a sentence? How many sentences make up a paragraph?" These questions allow students to compare what they've learned in other contexts and the instructor to clarify her expectations. Some of her students find that they use a particular strategy, though at first they didn't recognize the strategy's name, such as *MLA citation style*. Naming what students know can give them confidence and guide them to be more intentional in their writing. Moreover, when instructors understand students' writing backgrounds, their feedback can be more effective (Ambrose et al., 2010).

Applying principles of multicultural education (Banks, 2020), a linguistically inclusive grading approach draws on an equity pedagogy that adapts curriculum and instruction to the needs of all students. Susan, who previously taught high school, changes her lesson plans each semester based on each new group of students (Franz, 2019). She assigns students various readings to examine the structures at play in different written works, including patterns that some students may not have learned in high school.

In contrast with Susan's practices, many community college writing programs support remediation rather than curricular adaptation. A remediation approach often places responsibility on the individual student rather than systemic discriminatory practices and policies that have caused unequal writing preparation. A shared curriculum may expect specific skills from incoming students. If a student does not meet these expectations, the program or instructor might refer the student to a tutoring or writing center for extra help. Remediation may exacerbate inequities by requiring an unequal amount of extra work among students. For writing instructors who want to connect students to their campus's academic resources, a more inclusive approach would require all students to use at least one campus resource, provide options to accommodate different schedules, and directly reward these efforts. Instructors can invite writing center tutors or other academic support staff to the class to discuss their services and answer questions, thus embedding the support into the curriculum. Encouraging all students to use academic resources can challenge the association of academic support with remediation, lessening the stigma of seeking such feedback (Winograd & Rust, 2014).

Writing as Work and Revision

Writing instructors often want their students to engage in a whole writing process that includes revision rather than writing a paper the day it's due. Many composition courses embed stages of the writing process—including planning, peer feedback, and revising—into graded assignments. Some instructors allow students to revise as many times as the semester timeline allows to get the grade they want. Angela adopted these practices because of her belief that writing is about work rather than talent (Franz, 2019). She connects this belief to her understanding of unequal writing preparation, explaining that any student who puts in the work can succeed in her class, regardless of their previous writing experiences.

Composition scholar Inoue (2015) ties writing as work and revision to antiracist writing assessment. Specifically, to earn a B or above in the class, he tells students:

> When the job is to revise your thinking and work, you will reshape, extend, complicate, or substantially clarify your ideas—or relate your ideas to new things. You won't just correct, edit, or touch up. Revisions must somehow respond to or consider seriously your colleagues' (or teacher's) assessments in order to be revisions. (p. 334)

Inoue thus distinguishes substantial revisions from copy editing. If instructors assess writing based on the work put in, they may be more likely to avoid racial and linguistic bias.

Assessing writing based on work also prevents the scenario described previously in which only some students must seek extra help to succeed based on their educational background. Incorporating the writing process into assignments and grading can allow students to see writing as revision, in contrast to standardized test experiences that often require essays completed in one sitting.

INSTRUCTION IN ORGANIZATION AND GRAMMAR

Composition courses incorporate instruction in language use—organization, word choice, grammar, and mechanics—to different degrees and from different frameworks. Here, I compare several pairs of approaches to written language instruction. Many instructors probably use a combination of these approaches, but the comparisons can shed light on how to make the most of your practices to suit a linguistically inclusive grading approach.

Organization as Rhetorical Versus Organization as Formula

Reading is as critical as writing in many composition courses. A typical instructional approach has students analyze the choices of the writers they read, and this is one way to teach organization. Susan's students discuss the organizational structures of course readings (Franz, 2019). She finds that doing so helps her incoming students transition to college writing by learning new structures for writing. When students read, analyze, and evaluate different organizational styles, they are learning about linguistic variation. Students must have the opportunity to read and explore various organizational styles including African American English styles. For example, students may read narratives written in chronological order and narratives organized by topic, an African American English narrative style (Ball, 1996; Gilyard & Richardson, 2001). They can read analytical and argumentative works with an explicit thesis and works with an implied thesis (Ball & Lardner, 2005; Mosher, 2020). Understanding these styles from a reader's perspective can help them make rhetorical decisions as writers. A linguistically inclusive grading approach values these decisions as part of the grading process.

Another common instructional approach teaches students organizational formulas. While formulas can help students structure their writing, mandating a single formula can restrict students' rhetorical decision-making. Always requiring chronological order for narrative essays and an explicit thesis for argumentative papers can exclude African American English organizational styles. Instead, instructors can teach students to vary structures rhetorically. Chapter 5 provides several examples of effectively responding to organizational styles in a linguistically inclusive approach.

Grammar as Variation Versus Grammar as Error Correction

Following course objectives on rhetorical knowledge and critical thinking, composition instructors sometimes teach grammar and mechanics as variation or something that changes with the writer's tone, purpose, audience, and language variety (e.g., African American English). For instance, "the goal of code-meshing is to maximize (not minimize) rhetorical effectiveness. And the focus is on excellent communication rather than on how one adheres to prescribed grammar in one dialect" (Young et al., 2018). Grammar, like all language patterns, evolves. In contrast, instruction that teaches grammar as error correction can assume that grammar rules are fixed. Lunsford and Lunsford (2008) present the top 20 errors in first-year writing. A sociolinguistic perspective can reveal how these patterns are not always errors but sometimes sociolinguistic variations. Following, I explain how some of these top "errors" vary sociolinguistically. Chapter 6 further discusses these and other grammatical patterns.

Missing word. A missing word is one of the top errors listed in the Lunsford and Lunsford (2008) study. There are sociolinguistic variations that can look like missing words to instructors unfamiliar with those patterns. For example, in African American English, speakers aren't required to use *is* or *are*, since word order renders them redundant. So, the phrase *when you are done* in standardized English can also be *when you're done*, and in African American English, it can additionally be *when you done*. The meaning of *when you done* is evident from the order of the words, so *are* is not necessary for clarity. An instructor using a linguistically inclusive approach would treat this pattern as one of several options rather than as a random error. An instructor can describe these options (including contracting or excluding *is* or *are*) for students to teach the underlying pattern. This approach avoids devaluing African American English patterns as "missing."

Faulty sentence structure. Lunsford and Lunsford (2008) describe faulty sentence structures as those that confused instructors and caused them to pause. However, sentence structure varies between African American English and standardized English. Instructors unfamiliar with African American English sentence patterns might think that a particular sentence structure is faulty when it is, in fact, a rule-based pattern.

One example found in college student writing is a pattern known as an appositive pronoun or double subject. An appositive pronoun can clarify a complex subject to facilitate reading: *Tourists who are looking for beautiful beaches, they can. . . .* In this example, the pronoun *they* restates the long subject, reducing the chance that a reader will lose the subject as they read the sentence. A linguistically inclusive approach treats this pattern as one of two or more options for writing this sentence. An instructor using a linguistically inclusive approach might describe the following:

- The pattern: "This is a double subject, a pattern of African American English grammar."
- The pattern's function: "This pattern can help the reader follow or clarify a long subject."
- The standardized variation: "The standardized English version has just one subject, so *they* would not be used."

This approach avoids devaluing African American English patterns as "faulty." Even if your department requires that you prescribe particular grammar patterns, you can describe those patterns with this approach. An instructor unfamiliar with this African American English pattern might instead treat the appositive pronoun as an error. In this scenario, students might correct the sentence according to the instructor's directions but not understand the underlying pattern.

Unnecessary shift in verb tense. While Lunsford and Lunsford name verb tense shift as a frequent error, instructors can misread other patterns as a shift in tense. For example, variation in the suffix *–ed* is a spelling pattern related to African American English consonant cluster variation. In this pattern, a speaker might pronounce the word *gossiped* as *gossip*. This variation can be realized in student spelling so that the past tense form is likewise spelled *gossip*. Because this suffix indicates tense, instructors might respond to this pattern with comments such as "Make tense consistent." An instructor using a linguistically inclusive approach would use the following descriptions:

- The pattern: "Just like many speakers pronounce *and* as *an* in certain contexts, some speakers pronounce past tense forms like *gossiped* as *gossip* in certain contexts."
- The pattern's role in writing: "If you use this pronunciation, you might also use it in spelling."

This explanation avoids conflating pronunciation variation with tense shifts and treating this pattern as "unnecessary." This pattern is explained further in Chapter 6.

Frequently discussing grammar in terms of error can obscure the sociolinguistic nature of grammar. A linguistically inclusive approach describes grammar using words such as the following:

- Variation
- Patterns
- Options
- Language variety
- African American English
- Southern English

A linguistically inclusive approach *avoids* describing grammar in terms like the following:

- Error
- Correct/incorrect
- Right/wrong
- Faulty
- Missing
- Unnecessary

Note how the first set of terms can show value for African American English and other language varieties, while the second set places language varieties in a hierarchy. Think about how you might describe grammar in linguistically inclusive ways, even when you are aiming to teach standardized English patterns.

Treating grammar as variation does not mean that students don't have the opportunity to proofread for typos. Sometimes, *when you done* is sociolinguistic variation. Other times, the student may have left out *are* by mistake. Reading their work out loud can help students define and edit their own mistakes while maintaining the grammar patterns they meant to include. Instructors can take a linguistically inclusive approach to proofreading by situating possible edits in students' rhetorical choices:

> Variation in possessive form. "Obama style" can also be "Obama's style." Which pattern do you want to use here? Which suits your purpose of demonstrating the power of style-shifting?

Connecting grammar edits to a specific purpose or audience can reframe associations of African American English as error.

Instructors also teach grammar as variation when teaching how language varies by rhetorical situation. Stacey provides her classes with examples of language changing across genres and media, such as formal letters, emails, text messages, and voicemails (Franz, 2019). This instruction can prepare students to engage with linguistically inclusive feedback that asks them to analyze and evaluate their linguistic options. An important caveat to this type of instruction is to ensure that language varieties like African American English are not relegated to only informal genres. Assessment structures that restrict African American English to the informal assume that standardized varieties are superior (Charity Hudley, 2017; Lippi-Green, 2012). Instead, you can ask students to find examples of African American English in formal letters or academic writing, such as the writing of scholars Vershawn Ashanti Young (e.g., Young, 2010), April Baker-Bell (e.g., Baker-Bell et al., 2020), and Carmen Kynard (e.g., Kynard, 2007).

Grammar as Integral Versus Grammar as Add-On

Some composition instructors integrate grammar instruction throughout their courses. Susan prioritizes grammar as part of her students' transition to college writing (Franz, 2019). She wants her students to learn about grammar for effective communication and their credibility as writers. As a retired high school teacher, Susan understands students' prior writing experiences and aims to fill gaps in what they've encountered and what her composition program expects. Other instructors focus on different topics throughout the course and teach grammar and mechanics in brief sessions. Angela does not emphasize grammar in her class. Still, she conducts a copy-editing session for each writing assignment in response to the grammatical and mechanical issues she sees in student papers, such as run-on sentences (Franz, 2019). A former editor, Angela helps students polish their grammar and mechanics after spending class time on bigger-picture issues.

From an educational assessment perspective, instructors should consider and enact the relationship between curriculum, instruction, and assessment in their classrooms (Astin & Antonio, 2012; Bean, 2011), whether grammar is integral to their course or whether it is an add-on. Assessment guides instruction. Stacey uses her assessment of the grammar patterns in student writing to determine what patterns to emphasize in her grammar instruction for a particular class.

The relationship between assessment and instruction has implications for what instructors grade. If grammar and mechanics are integral to an instructor's grading, they should also be integral to their class instruction. If an instructor seldom features grammar and mechanics in class instruction, these features should play a small role in grading as well. Grading things that students don't have the opportunity to learn and practice in class can lead to grading based on students' educational backgrounds, which can create discriminatory barriers. A linguistically inclusive approach aims for equitable instruction by teaching the patterns instructors expect. If grammar and mechanics count for 10% on a rubric, is an equivalent proportion of class instruction devoted to these topics? If not, are there adjustments you can make? In many cases, writing instructors will want or need to continue to grade for grammar and mechanics, at least to some extent. In a linguistically inclusive approach, then, instructors may need to integrate more grammar instruction into their lessons. Moreover, students often wish for grammar instruction in their writing courses, as we found in our focus groups (Franz et al., 2022). It's important to note that ignoring grammar entirely does not support the causes of recognizing and valuing African American English, Southern English, and other language varieties. Delpit hits on this distinction:

> Progressive white teachers seem to say to their black students 'Let me help you find your voice. I promise not to criticize one note as you search for your song'. But the black teachers say 'I've heard your song loud and clear. Now I want to teach you to harmonize with the rest of the world.' (2006, p. 18)

The Black teachers Delpit describes address grammar and other language patterns and teach students to expand their linguistic repertoires.

ASSIGNMENT GOALS AND LANGUAGE VARIATION

The essay is a typical assignment in first-year writing. Essay assignments may be narrative, exposition, analysis, synthesis, review, argument, or research. Different instructors may have different specifications in mind when they assign the same type of essay. Many introductory composition courses gradually require more outside sources across the semester or a multiple-course sequence.

Different assignment types have different implications for students' language use and variation. When writing about their own experiences and culture, students tend to use more patterns from their own language variety (Perryman-Clark, 2013a). Literacy narratives, in particular, have been found to relate to the use of African American English or other specific language varieties not usually accepted in college writing (Perryman-Clark, 2013a). A linguistically inclusive grading approach rewards African American English or Southern English in narrative essays as part of a student's voice and necessary for students to tell their stories.

Aull (2020) found linguistic differences in first-year students' successful explanatory and argumentative writing. The argumentative papers that Aull analyzed had more grammatical variety and more in common with conversational writing than students' explanatory assignments. Specifically, the argumentative papers used more of the following:

- Generalized nouns (e.g., *people*)
- Generalized adverbs (e.g., *our time*)
- Dependent clauses (e.g., clauses starting with *because*)
- Boosters (e.g., *very*, *certainly*)
- Counters (e.g., *but*, *however*)
- Modals (e.g., *could*, *should*)
- Phrasal verbs (e.g., *bring up*, *come from*) (Aull, 2020)

Meanwhile, explanatory assignments were more grammatically dense, using long and complex subjects and other nouns, similar to published academic writing. Aull concludes that argumentative writing is more accessible for student writers.

A sample from a student's argumentative paper illustrates the patterns that Aull found:

> Unlike the 2000 Election, the 2008 Presidential Election was a historic election due to the story behind the candidates participating in it. For the first time in United States history, an African American was running for the most powerful office in the United States. Illinois Senator Barack Obama was a young, African American lawyer who was poised to be the first African American President. But he was not running unopposed. John McCain, the senior Senator from Arizona ran opposite of Obama. The story of these two candidates couldn't be any more different. Senator John McCain was an experienced politician serving his fourth term in Senate at the time. McCain was also a Navy Veteran who served in the Vietnam War. Obama on the other hand had just begun his first term as a United States Senator and had no prior military experience. Despite their differences, these two men ran in one of the most historic races in American history foreshadowing the most historic election outcome in history. (Franz et al., 2021)

This example uses generalizations ("For the first time in the United States," "couldn't be any more different"), dependent clauses ("who" clauses), boosters ("most"), counters ("but"), modals ("couldn't"), and phrasal verbs ("ran for"). These patterns may have more in common with conversational writing than published academic writing and can create a style that is more enjoyable to read. This student writer used African American English in both her speaking and writing, which contributed to her engaging style.

The following example, from a student writing an explanatory/synthesis assignment in a first-year writing course, demonstrates more grammatical density:

> However, the significance of the results of the previously mentioned study in relation to my experiences are limited due to the fact that the participants of the study were of "two different racial backgrounds" and were primed, or manipulated to identify with one of their parents (Gaither et al., p. 1). People that can identify with multiple social groups have an ability to "[adopt] specific cognitive strategies that enable them to associate more with one racial identity as needed" (Gaither et al., 2015, p. 8), which emphasizes that social identity can play a role in language production.

Note the long, complex nouns: "the significance of the results of the previously mentioned study in relation to my experiences" and "people that can identify with multiple social groups." This student followed the sentence patterns of the scholarly articles she read and cited. Even as students learn to write in this academic style, we can keep in mind that many find it boring to read!

Examine these different grammatical patterns: Do you comment on them in student writing? Do you reward or penalize them without comment? Look at some of your students' papers: Are you more likely to react positively to grammatical variety (as in the first example) or grammatical density (as in the second example)? Does the answer depend on the assignment? You may have some grammar expectations that you explain to students in assignment criteria or feedback but other grammar expectations may operate less consciously. It may be challenging to determine what grammar patterns you reward because we rarely provide specific positive feedback on grammar. And different instructors interpret the same grammar criterion differently. How do you operationalize "correct grammar," for example? And not just "incorrect grammar," which may be often easier to describe and exemplify. In a linguistically inclusive grading approach, it's important to learn what grammar patterns you favor so that you can ensure students have equitable opportunities to succeed. Doing so may mean making your expectations explicit or adjusting them to allow for more variation. Chapter 3 discusses positive comments and provides examples of specific positive comments on grammar and other micro-level linguistic features, and Chapter 6 gives specific examples of grammar patterns and how to respond to them in linguistically inclusive grading.

AUDIENCE

The intended audience for a piece of writing impacts what language patterns are effective for telling a story, making an argument, explaining a concept, or other assignment purposes. Audience design refers to the changes speakers and writers make to their linguistic style based on audience (Bell, 1984). Audience design includes both direct and indirect audiences. The instructor tends to be a direct audience in the writing classroom, but instructors can help students write to other readers and act as a more indirect audience themselves.

Assignments need to incorporate audience—who the student is to write to and how this audience is determined—in linguistically inclusive grading. Attention to audience supports course objectives on rhetorical knowledge. In my research, assignments described audiences as "a general adult public" or "an academic audience." Instructors should consider how students can use their own language when writing to such broad audiences. Keep in mind that a broad academic audience does not uniformly translate to strict standardized conventions. Black readers and African American English speakers need to be included as part of the general public and academic audiences. Instructors can reflect on whether they subconsciously assume a white audience and white linguistic norms when assigning a general or academic audience (Banks, 2011). For instance, before determining that a structure or phrase would confuse readers, use the African American English examples in the following chapters to learn how some audiences may read that structure or phrase. It's also crucial for instructors to reflect on who *they* write to when they write—what is the racial and linguistic identity of the readers you yourself write to? How do you address and reach multiple audiences with your own written work?

Redd (1995) found that students began to use more African American English rhetorical features, such as imagery and tonal semantics, when instructed to write to Black audiences. Tonal semantics create meaning, rhythm, and melodious qualities through sound effects (Smitherman, 1977). In writing, tonal semantics can be achieved through alliteration, rhyme, or other sound repetition (Gilyard & Richardson, 2001; Redd, 1995). When writing for a Black audience, Redd's student Gail used repetition to create a tonal rhythm:

> Education is the key, family is the key, values are the key to economic stability in the black community (p. 225)

Redd assigned students to write on the same topic for a white audience. Contrast Gail's tonal semantics with the same idea as she wrote it for a white audience:

> The Black family, knowledge, and values are keys to gain financial freedom. (p. 225)

Writing for a Black audience also allowed Gail to use lexical inclusion (Ball, 1992), that is, to directly incorporate her audience in her writing through pronouns such as *we*. Gail uses lexical inclusion to conclude her paper with a call to action for her and her Black readers:

> It may be hard but it can be done. We can thank our ancestors for showing us the way. (p. 225)

Redd explains that Gail's conclusion also uses phrasing reminiscent of gospel. In contrast, her paper for a white audience concludes with more distance from her topic through the use of *they* and *many*:

> The Black community must fall back on their ancestors strength for the courage to say "Yes I can," regardless of the ever present obstacles that face them such as the stereotypical attitudes of many in society. (p. 225)

From interviews with students, Redd learned that some student writers intentionally adapted their writing style based on the race of their intended audiences, whereas others seemed to adapt their style without being aware of why or how they were doing so. Feedback in a linguistically inclusive approach can point out stylistic patterns so students can gain metacognitive skills in varying their writing based on audience:

> Here, you use repetition to create a rhythm. In your future writing, decide how you want to use repetition to create this effect for your readers. This is a stylistic choice.

Making the audience as specific as possible can help students picture a real reader and make linguistic and other writing decisions accordingly. Students can draw on their knowledge of how their audience communicates to organize their papers and choose their vocabulary. Writing to a familiar audience can facilitate this process. In one assignment, Stacey had her students write to the college's students, faculty, and staff (Franz, 2019). If students' peers are among their audience, peer feedback takes on greater relevance. Students can have more confidence in providing feedback, knowing that it matters whether they specifically are convinced or entertained by their fellow students' writing. In this case, writing choices are no longer based on anticipating what the instructor wants but on a more authentic readership.

Assignments can give students the opportunity to determine their own audience. Ask students who they want to reach with their writing and why. This opportunity can increase the relevance of an assignment for students and, therefore, their motivation to learn to develop their writing (Ambrose et al., 2010). Practicing writing to different readers can prepare students for the range of readers they may encounter in their future work.

SELF-ASSESS YOUR PRACTICES

1. Do your course objectives, whether shared or individual, cover rhetorical knowledge or critical thinking? If so, how do you or how can you relate students' written language use to these objectives?
2. Do students have the opportunity to write in a variety of rhetorical situations? If so, do they have the chance to use a variety of language patterns, such as variation in organization, word choice, and grammar?
3. Do your course objectives, whether shared or individual, address writing conventions? If so, are conventions presented as fixed or dynamic?
4. Do students have the opportunity to analyze, evaluate, or create writing conventions?
5. Do your course objectives, whether shared or individual, refer to appropriateness? If so, who determines what counts as appropriate on a given assignment? Do students have the opportunity to decide what is appropriate based on multiple aspects of a rhetorical situation?
6. What types of writing do you aim to prepare students for? How do you learn the sociolinguistic details of these types of writing?
7. How do you prepare students to adapt to new writing situations?
8. How do you or how can you equitably support students when they have varying levels of writing preparation before your class?
9. Does your writing/composition program favor a remedial approach? How can you encourage all students, not just struggling students, to use academic resources?
10. Do you assign or allow revisions? Why and how?
11. How do you or can you directly reward students for their time and effort, including work put into revisions and time spent using academic resources?
12. How do you teach organization? Do you use course readings, formulas, other approaches?
13. Are students expected to apply a specific organizational structure to an individual assignment?
14. To what extent is grammar instruction part of your teaching? To what extent is it part of your grading? If there is a discrepancy, are there adjustments you can make?
15. Do you treat grammar as variation, as error correction, both, or something else?
16. Do you expect or reward different grammatical patterns in different assignment types? If so, do you explain these differences to students? Review some of your graded student papers to see any grammatical patterns that you may be rewarding subconsciously.
17. What is the racial and linguistic identity of the readers you yourself write to? How do you address and reach multiple audiences with your own written work?

18. Do your assignments specify an audience? If so, are Black audiences and African American English speakers included? Do students have the opportunity to determine the audience they want to reach?

LINGUISTICALLY INCLUSIVE PRACTICES

1. Comment on students' language variation based on rhetorical situations such as the audience or purpose.
2. Frame appropriateness objectives so students have an opportunity to determine what language features are appropriate, including based on their voice.
3. Encourage students to analyze, evaluate, and create rather than just apply writing conventions.
4. Gather information about what students are writing in other courses. You can directly ask them and your colleagues in other departments about writing assignments.
5. Develop students' metacognition by drawing their attention to how and why they and other writers make decisions about their writing.
6. Encourage all students to use academic resources by incorporating them into your curriculum and in-class instruction.
7. Incorporate stages of the writing process, such as peer feedback or revisions, into assignments.
8. Have students analyze and evaluate the organizational structures of course readings. Use these evaluations to teach students to vary organizational styles rhetorically.
9. Describe language using terms such as variation, patterns, styles, options, language variety, African American English, and Southern English.
10. Ask students to find examples of African American English in formal letters or academic writing.
11. Situate copy editing in audience, purpose, and voice.
12. Teach grammar as more than error correction.
13. Align the time you devote to grammar in class with its role in your grading.
14. Once you've determined what language patterns you may be subconsciously rewarding, make those expectations explicit for students or adjust your expectations to allow for more language variation. Use the examples throughout this book to provide explicit descriptions as feedback.
15. Include Black audiences and African American English speakers in the audiences that students write to.
16. Refer to audience in assignment descriptions.
17. Ask students who they want to reach with their writing.

CHAPTER 3

Linguistically Inclusive Grading Processes

How do you assign a grade or other final evaluation on a student's paper? What goes into that process for you? This chapter focuses primarily on summative assessment—the evaluation an instructor gives a student's paper, especially the final evaluation. Summative assessment, the more literal part of "grading," might incorporate letter grades, number grades, points, rubrics, checklists, or a complete/incomplete. This final evaluation may be based on a single version of a student's paper or may factor in the writing process via multiple drafts or peer feedback. Students often must learn and adapt to new grading processes across their classes. In one class, students might receive a letter grade and a qualitative checklist that indirectly relates to the grade. In another class, students might receive a final score out of a maximum amount that is directly based on a numerical rubric. This chapter will help you reflect on and explain your grading processes, which may seem straightforward to you but may be new to some of your students. Crucially, this chapter exemplifies practices for grading and evaluation in a linguistically inclusive approach.

CONSIDER GRADING PRIORITIES AND DISTRIBUTION

Consider what features of a student's paper are most important to you when determining their grade, why, and in what order. Your priorities probably vary by assignment. Features that might be important on any given assignment include purpose; thesis; analysis or synthesis; word choice; grammar and mechanics; and the structure of the paper, paragraphs, or sentences. If you assign multiple drafts and revisions, you may prioritize how much the student revised or responded to specific feedback. You may have late policies or other assignment submission guidelines that can greatly impact the grade. If your department mandates a percentage-based rubric, your grading priorities may be largely determined for you. If you use contract grading or another holistic grading approach, you may still have criteria you use for individual assignments to determine whether they are sufficient for the terms of the grading contract.

As an exercise, choose a few of your common or representative assignments and try to rank your grading criteria from the most to least important. If you or your department assigns percentages to grading criteria, this exercise may seem straightforward, although there may be more nuance in your actual grading than in the listed criteria. Read your feedback and grades on several papers to determine what was actually prioritized when the final letter, number, or other evaluation was assigned. It may be helpful to look at all the papers with the highest grades and see not only what is similar across the student writing but also across your comments or rubric ratings. You can then do the same for all the papers with the lowest grades. I encourage you to try to put aside any assumptions when trying this exercise. You may be surprised to find that on a particular assignment or even a few individual papers, your priorities shift.

Adapt the following questions to your current grading system:

1. When reading papers with the highest evaluation, what do you notice that they have in common? Try to find at least one feature that you may not have expected or previously noticed.
2. What is similar about your comments (including rubric or checklist ratings) across the most highly evaluated papers?
3. Repeat 1 and 2 for papers with the lowest evaluation.
4. What are the nonnegotiable features of a paper with your highest grade or evaluation?
5. If you use contract, portfolio, or holistic grading, what features of the paper are most important for determining whether that paper can contribute to a final grade of an A or a B at the end of the term?
6. Are there different ways to earn a high evaluation on the same assignment? If so, what are they?
7. What features, if any, automatically lead a paper to receive a low evaluation? Are these features you teach in class or features you expect students to have learned previously?
8. Do low evaluations help your students improve?
9. Use your responses to the questions 1 through 8 to rank your grading priorities.

It may be helpful to reflect on your grade distribution in addition to your grading priorities. Figure 3.1 shows the grading distribution of each instructor in my study (Franz, 2019). The figure reflects the number of major papers receiving each letter grade in a single section of a composition course. Looking at the three different grade distributions, what stands out to you? How do you think each grade distribution reflects the instructor's goals? One of Angela's goals was to encourage students to continue to revise for a higher grade, so you can see that reflected in the high number of low

Figure 3.1. Grade distribution for each instructor in the study

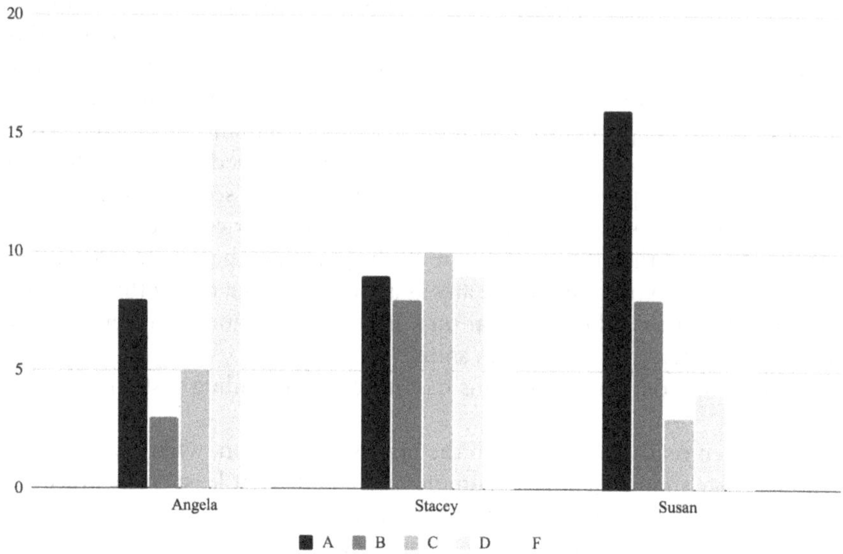

grades. The next question for Angela to ask would be whether her strategy is working and actually encouraging students to revise and receive a higher grade. One of Susan's goals, meanwhile, was to grade students only on writing strategies that they had practiced in class, reflected in her high number of high grades. You can consider what your own grade distribution looks like for a set of papers and why, and how your grade distribution supports student learning:

- What is your goal in assigning an A or other high evaluation?
- What is your goal in assigning a D, F, or other low evaluation?
- Does your grade distribution help you meet your priorities for student learning?

Remember from Chapter 1 that grades have very real consequences for students.

ALIGN GRADING PRIORITIES WITH INSTRUCTION

As discussed in Chapter 2, a linguistically inclusive grading approach works best when curriculum, instruction, and assessment are aligned. This alignment supports student learning and equitable pedagogical practices. For instance, Susan grades student papers based on the writing strategies she has modeled in class and taught during the revision process (Franz, 2019). Susan's extensive high school teaching experience likely influences these connections between grading and instruction; K–12 best practices recommend explicitly tying assessment to instruction to promote student learning (Gareis & Grant, 2015). Susan models a specific type of writing several times before she grades that writing type. She also allows students to practice the writing strategies modeled by assigning two rough drafts graded for completion before officially grading the final draft. On these rough drafts, students receive peer feedback on the writing strategies learned in class. Susan uses detailed rubrics to teach students how to give peer feedback. When grading the final drafts, Susan uses similar rubrics and only deducts points in areas that she introduced in class. Susan's alignment of teaching and grading contrasts with models in which instructors grade based, wholly or in part, on what they think students should have learned already and do not teach themselves. Her effort to connect grading directly to her class instruction can thus help prevent grading based on students' educational backgrounds. This effort is vital in seeking justice in grading.

Once you've ranked your own grading priorities, consider how they match priorities in your curriculum and instruction:

- Are your highest-ranked grading priorities also your most important learning objectives?
- Are your highest-ranked grading priorities also the areas you spend the most time teaching?
- If you notice any misalignment, how can you make changes—to your grading, objectives, or teaching—that help you grade what you (or your department) value and teach?

In considering these questions, maybe you find that you are grading what you expect students to have learned prior to your class even when they haven't learned those things. In this case, remember that one college term is not enough time to make up for years of gaps in secondary education. And these gaps will not be remedied by low grades for what students weren't taught in high school. Grading students for what they haven't learned will exacerbate educational inequities and may even encourage them to use mechanisms like generative AI without benefiting their writing development. Instead, adjust your grading, teaching, or both to align with each other. In my years of working in secondary and college writing contexts, including classrooms and academic support programs, I have encountered few educators who *want* to teach grammar. Some say it's not their job to do so. Yet, most want their students to know about written grammar. This incongruity doesn't help students. If you observe this issue in your context, add some grammar instruction into your teaching or perhaps shift away from grammar in your grading.

If you have mandated grade weights, they may conflict with your individual values for teaching writing to students. However, you may still be able to make adaptations in line with your values. Say you value linguistic flexibility and diversity, whereas your department mandates grading based on academic conventions across assignments. In that case, you may be able to broaden the definition of academic conventions to include the academic value of varieties such as African American English. Or, you can adapt your teaching to ensure you are teaching the graded academic conventions from a linguistically inclusive perspective, placing academic language as one option among many and on equal footing with other language varieties.

Next, reflect on how your grading priorities and their rationale are communicated to students. Do students know what they need to prioritize to be successful on each assignment? Do they know why? Sometimes, students may have misconceptions about how their papers are graded based on their prior experiences. Some incoming college students may have learned, explicitly or implicitly, to associate writing with formal correctness. If, like the instructors in my study, you usually prioritize purpose, you would want to explain from the outset how this priority should influence students' work and process. Different instructors also operationalize the same grading criteria in different ways. When you give students a new writing assignment, take the time to explain to students what you are actually grading when you grade each criterion, even if your department mandates a percentage-based rubric that seems self-explanatory. For some instructors, grading priorities shift across assignments. In a linguistically inclusive grading approach, it is important to explain these shifts and how they support students' writing development or particular curriculum objectives.

In my study, the instructors who did not use percentage-based rubrics made comments that explained the student's grade and how to improve for a higher grade (Franz, 2019):

- What can improve the grade to an A level is focusing a little more on *persuading* the reader why they should seriously consider joining this fandom. You do a good job describing what the fandom is and why it's special, but some sentences directed toward persuading the readers to join it would help satisfy the purpose of the article.
- This article is a great start; it's still in the advanced rough draft stage. . . . It mostly needs to expand on the descriptions and especially on the analysis sections, so that you're really getting across all the ways that these ads are persuading the readers emotionally and psychologically. I am happy to guide you further on this if you'd like to revise it for a higher grade, which I encourage.
- I feel strongly that you can bring this up to an A grade if you can refocus your description and analysis for the second ad and resubmit it. Keep moving forward!

This information can help the student see the instructor's priorities. Importantly, students should also be guided in how to apply these priorities prior to working on their assignment. Angela also calls her assignments "articles" and provides a list of what to improve for the next revision in priority order, much like the peer review process for academic journal articles.

Even if your institution uses something other than traditional letter grades, such as satisfactory/unsatisfactory or a more qualitative assessment, as long as there is some type of end-of-term evaluation, students should have the opportunity to learn how their individual writing assignments will contribute to that evaluation. Explain how grades will be assigned even if you use a method, like contract grading, in which individual assignments are not graded. In this way, you ensure that students have what they need to succeed in your class.

As a final exercise in grading priorities, it may be useful to compare your quantity of comments on different writing features with your rankings of priorities. For example, in my study, I found that mechanics was the most frequently commented-on feature across participants (see Figure 6.1), despite the fact that mechanics was not a top grading priority for most assignments. Such a discrepancy could give mixed messages to students as to what they should prioritize to improve their grade and their writing in the class. It may be helpful to instead align your comments with your grading priorities.

READ FOR STUDENT MEANING

In a linguistically inclusive approach, an instructor reads student work with the goal of understanding the student's meaning (see Himley & Carini, 2000; Redd & Webb, 2005). By reading for student meaning, instructors can avoid unintentionally penalizing students for African American English or Southern English structures that they may not recognize. The instructor actively tries to make sense of student work by acknowledging their own subjectivity as a reader, stating what they think the student means, and posing questions, rather than penalties, when they don't understand:

> I had to read this sentence a few times to understand it. I think you're saying____. Do you think this sentence would be better reworded, or do you think your target audience is more familiar with this sentence structure?

Our mandated grading structures tend to compel us to read for evaluation. And time constraints often mean that we *only* have time to read for evaluation. We may have time to read each student's paper just once and thus have to immediately read with a mind toward the grade. Fortunately, with a little reframing, reading for student meaning can be adapted to a busy schedule and to the need to evaluate and assign grades. Here are some questions you can ask as you read a student's paper that you're having trouble understanding:

- What do I think the student is trying to say? To who? Why?
- Am I having difficulty understanding the main ideas or just some sentences? If it's just some sentences, how can I focus the grade on other areas, like the assignment purpose?
- If I'm having trouble understanding the main ideas, what do I need to ask in my comments to grade this paper based on the assignment purpose or other areas? Can I give the student an opportunity to resubmit the paper, addressing my questions?

Keep in mind that truly reading for student meaning is different from simply claiming to not understand what a student is saying. The latter is what Coleman et al. (2016), quoted more extensively in Chapter 1, describes when a writing instructor's feedback conveyed "that she could not understand what I was writing because it did not make any sense" (p. 367). Here, the writing instructor is not taking on her share of the burden of communication (Lippi-Green, 2012). In a linguistically inclusive approach, an instructor reads for student meaning as a way to share this burden—there is a focus on questions and the instructor's subjectivity.

USE AND EXPLAIN SOCIOLINGUISTICALLY INFORMED GRADING CRITERIA

Sociolinguistically informed grading criteria take into account the variation that is inherent in all language, particularly written language. Such criteria imply that language choices are influenced by a range of factors and that there is no one right way to write. For example, writing instructor and scholar Dr. Michelle Grue (2020) grades on criteria such as whether "[w]riting mechanics [is] informed by context." Grue's rubric descriptor for an A in this category lists the contextual factors that she expects to inform students' linguistic choices:

> Grammar, mechanics, and sentence-level writing reflect the purpose, message, and audience of the piece.

Similar criteria can be applied to other language-based grading priorities, such as organization and word choice:

- Transitions reflect your voice and purpose
- Use of pronouns/person engage your audience
- Word choice supports informing your audience

- "The style of the prose speaks to the content, purpose, and audience and is maintained throughout the writing" (Muhammad, 2020, p. 94)
- "The piece is interesting and keeps the writer engaged" (Muhammad, 2020, p. 94)

These criteria focus on student writers' options and intentions, rather than errors, aligning with a translingual approach to writing support (Shapiro & Del Russo, 2023). To meet these criteria, students have to understand, analyze, and evaluate the choices available to them for transitions, pronouns, and other language patterns. Specifically, students must consider the rhetorical context of their writing to meet these criteria: Who am I writing to? Why? What do I want them to take away from my work? How can I draw on and cultivate my individual writing style? These questions make space for students to use and develop their own voice, including African American English and other language varieties, as part of being a successful writer. In a linguistically inclusive approach, students do not have to compromise their language and voice to get good grades.

In these examples, grading criteria do not necessitate that every student uses the same grammar patterns, transition types, pronouns, or word choices. Instead, the criteria guide the instructor to assess these features contextually. When assessing sociolinguistic descriptors, instructors can indicate the connections they see between the student's linguistic choices and their audience, purpose, or voice. You can use the following template as a starting point to create these comments: "[Language pattern] gives your paper a [nonevaluative descriptor] tone/style/quality that [relationship to] your audience/purpose/voice":

- The repeated phrases give your paper a rhythmic quality that aligns with your purpose to discuss the values of poetry.
- Generalizations ("for the first time," "most people") give your paper a conversational style that can engage your audience.
- Long subjects/nouns give your paper a tone similar to the technical articles you are synthesizing.

Some sociolinguistically informed grading criteria refer directly to African American English or other language varieties. For example, on Dr. Grue's (2020) rubric, the descriptor for the highest evaluation for word choice includes the following:

> Word choice is sophisticated in its experimentation and shows consideration of using Black/African American Vernacular English, among other dialects and languages other than English, as appropriate.

Meanwhile, more traditional grading criteria imply one right writing style, a uniform audience, and language as static: "Transitions are logical;"

"Pronouns are clear and mostly third person"; "Paper is readable." In contrast to the linguistically inclusive approach, such criteria have several disadvantages. Terms like *logical*, *clear*, and *readable* are often confined to standardized English and exclude effective African American English patterns. So, many students are compelled to sacrifice their own voice for a good grade. In a linguistically inclusive grading approach, criteria must account for the logic and clarity of African American English patterns. Meanwhile, to meet traditional grading criteria, students largely have to understand and apply conventions rather than use higher-level critical thinking skills. When decisions about transitions and pronouns are made for students, they do not have to develop as deep of an understanding of their rhetorical situation.

Different instructors, even in the same program or department, have different expectations as they assign and evaluate writing. This point is important to remember when going over grading or other criteria for students' writing. Students may assume that they are being graded the same way they were last year or last term, and instructors may assume that students have been graded based on the same criteria used in their own classes. Students in our focus groups (Franz et al., 2022) described these experiences:

- Because some of my classmates have other experiences, when I say, "My professor . . . just wants to hear my voice," [my peers are like,] "Are we going to the same school?"
- High school was very structured: If you want this grade, do this writing. There's not a voice that you hear. All student papers would be the same. In college, you're picking what you want to write about and writing in a way that's comfortable for you. "You mean you want me to write what I want to write?" The professor said, "I want to hear your own voice," and I was like, "What did that even mean?"

When students have been taught that there is one way to write in school and when their own voice has been continually corrected, it can take time for them to understand what an instructor means by *voice*. Hankerson (2017) demonstrates how students contend with this contradiction and provides activities for teaching voice. In a linguistically inclusive grading approach, instructors explain grading criteria and connect criteria to class instruction so that students understand how expectations may or may not differ from how they've been graded in the past. If you want to hear students' voices, you can explain what that looks like:

> You will be writing to me but also to other readers. Think beyond what you may have been taught is "good writing" or "academic writing." Instead, work on writing to your readers in ways that they will find engaging. You can maintain your individual writing style through your word choice and how you arrange your sentences and writing overall.

You can also refer students to Purdue OWL's (2022) section on "Creating Your Persona," which explains other ways to consider voice:

> A writer's persona communicates to their audience who they are. It's not only a chance to give writing a little personality, it is also an opportunity for writers to connect to readers by allowing them to imagine the person who wrote the text they're now reading (or the character narrating that text). A writer's persona doesn't need to encompass every single aspect of who they are as a person—rather, it's a way of presenting a coherent identity to their readers through their language. (para 1)

Subsequent sections on Purdue OWL explain that both word choice and sentence structure can be a part of a writer's persona or style.

Students can discuss their perceptions of grading criteria using reading assignments. Susan has her students read writing in the form she is looking for so that they know what to work on (Franz, 2019). In a linguistically inclusive approach, it's important to include multiple examples that exhibit variation in organization, word choice, or grammar. The *Students' Right to Their Own Writing* guide (srtow.org) provides a list of published works across genres that use African American English in different ways. Works include the following:

- "Very Smart Brothas—Black News, Opinions, Politics and Culture" column in *The Root* (nonfiction)
- *Well-Read Black Girl: Finding our Stories, Discovering Ourselves* by Glory Edim (2018) (a mix of nonfiction and fiction)
- *Imani All Mine* by Connie Porter (1999) (fiction)
- *The Hate U Give* by Angie Thomas (2017) (fiction)

Muiru (2021) and Okonkwo (2021) also list written works that draw on the skill and beauty of African American English.

To explain grading criteria through student discussion, pose questions to students about the texts they're asked to read:

- How did the writer organize the piece? Chronologically? Thematically? Divided by headings? In one long flow? How does the organization reflect the writer's purpose, audience, or voice?
- How does the writer convey their main point(s)? Directly? Implied? How does this approach reflect the writer's purpose, audience, or voice?
- How would you describe the writer's word choice? Technical? Conversational? Rhythmic? How does the word choice reflect the writer's purpose, audience, or voice?
- How would you describe the writer's sentence structure? Simple? Complex? African American English grammar? How does this sentence structure reflect the writer's purpose, audience, or voice?

Non-evaluative descriptors, like *chronological*, *implied*, *technical*, and *rhythmic*, will be most helpful for students. More value-laden terms in writing assessment, like *logical*, *clear*, *informal*, and *proper*, are less likely to give students the picture they need because they are more culturally mediated. The value-laden terms also suggest that there is one correct way to write, whereas the nonevaluative terms provide options for students to choose from. Sociolinguistically informed grading criteria are about variation, so they need to be explained with examples of what that variation can look like and why.

WORD GRADING CRITERIA POSITIVELY

After you have made sure your grading criteria are sociolinguistically informed, it's also crucial to word those criteria positively, defining what you do expect, and not in terms of what you *don't* expect. Positively worded criteria can help students see when and how they meet those expectations, especially when the criteria are specific as well as positive. In our research team's focus groups, students explained that in some classes, they receive little feedback on their A papers (Franz et al., 2022). The students wanted to learn more about what they did well when they received a good grade. If grading criteria describe the features that make a successful paper, students can have a framework for understanding what they do well. In my study (Franz, 2019), Angela described grading students on what they do well by positively wording her criteria (see Table 3.1). Angela's positively worded criteria revolve around content more than language. Language-based criteria can sometimes be more difficult to convey positively. In my study, language-based criteria were more likely to be worded negatively than content-based criteria, though it is important to word both positively. It becomes more

Table 3.1. Positively Versus Negatively Worded Grading Criteria

Positively Worded Grading Criteria	Negatively Worded Grading Criteria
• Has descriptive title • Begins in a way that suits the paper's purpose • Structures the paper to engage readers • Uses ample description • Uses word choice and sentence structure to create the intended tone • Uses verb endings that reflect audience, purpose, and voice	• Avoids extensive summary • Avoids topic shifts • No unclear wording • No run-on sentences • No errors in subject–verb agreement • No misuse of modifiers

difficult for students to understand how they are meeting these criteria that refer to what the paper lacks rather than what it does.

Positively worded criteria can support students in meeting your expectations, particularly when those criteria are sociolinguistically informed and aligned with class instruction. Say you have been discussing verb endings in class and would like to support students in this area on a particular assignment. You could word this criterion in several ways. If you expect students to think critically about rhetorical variation, a positive, sociolinguistically informed criterion might be:

> Uses verb endings that reflect audience, purpose, and voice: verb forms specific to African American English (no endings on verbs with third-person singular subjects such as *it*, *she*, or *he*) or verb forms used in African American English and standardized English (-*s* endings for verbs with subjects such as *it*, *she*, or *he*)

This criterion not only pairs a specific language pattern—verb endings—with the rhetorical situation but also explicitly describes how this pattern might vary based on rhetorical factors. This description can thus reiterate lessons from the classroom. The positive wording communicates high expectations for student writers while guiding them on how to meet those expectations (see Cohen et al., 1999).

If, on a particular assignment, your goal is for students to use solely standardized English forms, it remains important to word that expectation positively and specifically in a linguistically inclusive approach:

> Present tense verbs end in -*s* for third-person singular subjects, such as *it, she,* or *he* or words that can be replaced by *it, she,* or *he.*

This criterion tells students what their writing should look like rather than what it should not look like, and describes the specific language pattern. The negatively worded version, "No errors in subject–verb agreement," gives students less information to apply directly to their writing. The positive version that is less sociolinguistically informed, "Subjects and verbs agree," similarly provides little linguistic detail.

MAXIMIZE PEER FEEDBACK AND MULTIPLE DRAFTS

Historically, many Black writers valued reshaping their writing in response to peer feedback (Muhammad, 2020). Members of Black literacy societies of the 19th century provided each other with feedback to refine their writing for the audiences they wanted to reach (Muhammad, 2020). If you use peer feedback in your teaching, make this an opportunity for students to learn from multiple audiences as they continue to cultivate their voice and expand their linguistic repertoire. Peer feedback can allow students to discover how readers other than writing instructors respond to their content and language choices. As high school English teacher Mrs. Kirsten Bradley shared, teaching students to use peer feedback in this way requires a shift for students who have learned to equate revising with surface-level correction (Franz et al., 2022). Mrs. Bradley explained that students need practice and specific prompts to encourage them to read their classmates' work for impact rather than for spelling and mechanical errors.

Like instructors, students can focus on reading each other's paper for meaning over evaluation. Students can provide feedback on what they understand their peer's paper to say by responding to prompts such as the following:

- Summarize your partner's paper in five sentences.
- Summarize your partner's paper in two sentences.
- Reverse outline (i.e., outlining a paper that has already been written) your partner's paper or draw a mind map or other representation of the paper that combines text with visuals.
- What are you most likely to remember about your partner's paper? Why?
- What would you say was your partner's main goal or purpose in this paper?
- What audience is your partner trying to reach? Who do you think should read this paper?

Students can use this feedback from their peers to learn how a reader understands their meaning and purpose. If their classmate did not take away the message that the writer wanted them to, the writer can make a plan to revise. Because many students may be new to revising in this way, prompts can be useful at this stage as well:

- What did your partner get out of reading your paper?
- Are there any important points that your partner seemed to have missed? If so, how might you emphasize these points? Talk to your partner about your ideas.
- Are there any points that your partner seemed to have interpreted differently from what you intended? If so, how might you reframe or reword these points? Talk to your partner about your ideas.
- Did your partner get something out of your paper that you did not expect? If so, would you like other readers to take away this point as well? Consider whether you would like to further emphasize or de-emphasize this point.
- Does your partner's reverse outline follow the flow you were going for? If not, how might you reorganize your paper?

This peer feedback model supports a linguistically inclusive grading approach with emphasis on the social context of writing. Students are interacting with their peers as readers rather than editors to learn about the why of revising rather than just about the what or how. In this way, students are better positioned to make their own linguistic choices as writers. And if students are using generative AI to assist with their writing process or product, these peer feedback and revision questions can help them give more informed prompts to the AI tool.

In peer feedback sessions, students can also be assigned to read their papers aloud to each other. The goal is for students to catch their own mistakes and, importantly, define mistakes according to their own language patterns. Students can then be graded on evidence of their proofreading edits ("What did you change when you read your paper aloud?") instead of a narrow set of conventions that may disadvantage African American English speakers and writers.

If your students receive feedback from you on a first draft, whether or not they receive peer feedback, you can adapt some of the peer feedback prompts to support a linguistically inclusive grading approach. You can do this even if you offer minimal feedback on first drafts. For example, your feedback may simply state, "I understand your main purpose to be . . ." or "I would summarize your paper in one sentence as . . . ," followed by "If I seemed to have misinterpreted your main purpose, how can you reframe or reword your purpose throughout your paper?" Instructor feedback on first drafts is also a great opportunity to provide the type of critical feedback that has been found to be motivating for Black college students (Cohen et al., 1999). Angela often followed her suggestions for improvement on early drafts with comments such as:

> Recommended for revision. This has the potential for a much higher grade. Keep moving forward!

This comment couches constructive criticism in confidence that the student can improve (Cohen et al., 1999).

Ensure that students understand how multiple drafts and revisions fit into their grades, if at all. Writing instructors vary regarding whether they require, grade, or give comments on first drafts. Therefore, your students may be accustomed to different grading and feedback approaches throughout the writing process. A student used to instructor feedback on first drafts might need instruction on revising when the instructor does not give first-draft feedback or does not assign multiple drafts. A student used to revising for a higher grade may be more focused on writing for a grade than for any other purpose. Explain to students your rationale and system for grading and commenting on first drafts, final drafts, further revisions, or other parts of the writing process so that all students have a chance to succeed within your model.

POSE QUESTIONS RATHER THAN PENALTIES

In your grading, consider strategic questions as an alternative to grade penalties for language forms that may seem informal, confusing, or unfamiliar to you. Questions allow instructors to look for intention instead of error (Shapiro & Del Russo, 2023). Unlike point deductions, in a linguistically inclusive grading approach, questions can open up a conversation between the student and instructor and present the opportunity for students to make more thoughtful revisions or improve their next assignment and thus write for more than a grade. Questions can also help instructors avoid penalizing students for the use of their own language. For example, instead of penalizing students for an "unclear thesis," ask, "What is your primary purpose? Do you want to state your purpose for your audience or have them infer it?" Instead of penalizing students for a disorganized paper, ask, "How might you reorganize your paper to make sure your reader takes away the points you want them to?"

In my research, I found that point deductions for criteria such as "readability" penalized students for patterns of African American English and Southern English. African American students and other students may use sentence structures that they believe are readable to teachers (Hankerson, 2017). When instructors penalize students for these usages, students can become further confused about what the instructor wants and why (Hankerson, 2017). Such practices force many Black students to work harder than some of their peers to be successful in the class based on their language. A linguistically inclusive grading approach seeks to address such injustices; instead of penalizing students for "unreadable sentences," ask, "Is there another way you might word this? Or do you think your audience will be more familiar than I am with this sentence structure?" Questions allow students to clarify their meaning and make their own decisions. Chapter 4 discusses questions as feedback in more depth, while Chapters 5 and 6 will help you learn about written African American English patterns.

SELF-ASSESS YOUR PRACTICES

1. How often do you give student papers As? Why?
2. How often do you fail student papers? Why?
3. What distinguishes an A paper from a B paper in your class? What is the role of language patterns in this distinction?
4. What distinguishes a passing paper from a failing paper in your class? What is the role of language patterns in this distinction?
5. Are your highest-ranked grading priorities also the areas you spend the most time teaching? If you notice any misalignment, what changes can you make to help you grade what you teach?

6. Do expectations of what students should have already learned play a role in your grading? If so, what adjustments can you make to grade students for what they have learned rather than what they haven't learned?
7. How does your grading of student writing compare to that of your colleagues? If there are differences, how do you think these differences impact students?
8. How did you learn how to grade?
9. How did you learn how to give comments on student papers?
10. Do your students know what aspects of their writing to prioritize to get the grade they want on an assignment?
11. Are rubric categories and other grading criteria described in positive terms (what you want to see) or negative terms (what you don't want to see)?
12. If you refer to voice, style, or persona in your grading criteria, do your students know what this means? (See Purdue OWL, 2022, for ideas.)
13. Do all your students understand what you mean by the language patterns listed in rubrics and other grading criteria? Do they know how to apply these language patterns to their writing? Examples include "logical transitions," "clear wording," and "subject–verb agreement."
14. If you assign first drafts, do students understand how to revise these first drafts to get a particular grade?
15. If you use peer feedback, what type of feedback do students give their peers? How do they learn how to give feedback? (See Franz et al., 2022 for ideas.)

LINGUISTICALLY INCLUSIVE PRACTICES

1. Determine your grading priorities.
2. If your students submit multiple versions of an assignment, explain to them your rationale for grading and commenting on first drafts, final drafts, further revisions, or other parts of the writing process. Your students may be accustomed to different grading and feedback approaches throughout the writing process, so make sure they understand your system.
3. Explain to students how you will prioritize different aspects of writing as you grade their papers.
4. Explain criteria like voice, style, and persona. Use resources like Purdue OWL (2022).
5. Replace "readability" and "clarity" as language grading criteria with contextualized criteria related to language patterns you specifically taught in class.

6. Read papers to understand student meaning rather than to penalize sentence structures you don't immediately recognize.
7. Replace rubric descriptors that present language as fixed with those that acknowledge language as variable. For example, replace "clear" and "logical" with "suits your audience, purpose, and voice."
8. Explain the connection between the student's linguistic choices and their audience, purpose, or voice so that students can tell how you're using criteria to grade specific aspects of their writing. You can use this template: [Language pattern] gives your paper a [non-evaluative descriptor] tone/style/quality that [relationship to] your audience/purpose/voice.
9. Word grading criteria positively, in terms of what you do expect rather than in terms of what you do not expect (see Table 3.1).
10. Explicitly describe the language patterns you expect in your grading criteria. Use the examples in this and the following chapters.
11. If you use peer feedback in your teaching, take advantage of that time to have students give each other feedback on what they understand their peer's paper to be saying.
12. If you use peer feedback, have students read their papers aloud to each other to define mistakes according to their own language patterns.
13. Use prompts to guide students' revisions in response to peer or instructor feedback. You can also use prompts to encourage students' informed use of generative AI in the writing process.
14. If you give minimal feedback on first or final drafts, focus your feedback on what you notice about your top grading priority.
15. Pose questions instead of penalties for language patterns that may seem informal, confusing, or unfamiliar to you.
16. Use the following chapters to learn about African American English patterns in student writing to avoid penalizing those patterns.

CHAPTER 4

Linguistically Inclusive Commenting Strategies

When you read student papers, how do you decide what to comment on? What do you want students to get out of your comments? This chapter explains linguistically inclusive strategies for making summative and formative comments on student papers. Although different instructors use different commenting strategies, as I explain in this chapter, my research found corrections, labels, and uncontextualized prescriptive comments to be the most common strategies. Meanwhile, as shown in Table 4.1, linguistically inclusive comments are specific descriptions and questions that provide context, highlight the instructor's subjectivity, and acknowledge multiple audiences. Questions, specificity, and context are more likely to communicate high expectations and to motivate linguistic agency, rhetorical knowledge, and critical thinking than traditional comments. This chapter provides the tools for you to accomplish these teaching goals with written comments.

Table 4.1. Commenting Strategies in a Linguistically Inclusive Approach

Linguistically Inclusive Approach	Traditional Approach
Uses feedback as a conversation	Uses feedback to evaluate or justify a grade
Makes positive comments specific	Leaves positive comments general ("good")
Provides specific description	Labels features of students' writing
Asks questions about students' choices	Corrects features of students' writing, including African American English and Southern English
Contextualizes prescriptive comments to help students understand feedback	Tells students what to change but may exclude how and why
Highlights the instructor's subjectivity as a reader	Frames comments as nonnegotiable conventions
Acknowledges multiple audiences	Assumes only a white, standardized-English-speaking audience

REAPPORTION YOUR TIME

As summarized in Table 4.1, a linguistically inclusive approach to comments may appear more time-consuming than a traditional approach. Corrections, labels, and general positive comments seem efficient—experienced graders can quickly mark dozens of papers in this way. For instructors teaching 50, 75, or 100 students per term, specific comments, questions, and added context likely feel like luxuries they cannot afford. In fact, linguistically inclusive comments can work—and be more efficient than traditional comments—for instructors with large teaching loads.

In a linguistically inclusive grading approach, instructors reapportion their grading time based on their priorities. A linguistically inclusive approach can help you increase the quality of your comments by engaging the student in your feedback and, if necessary, reduce the quantity of your comments. For each assignment, ask yourself what your top priority is. Remember from Chapter 3 that you will want this priority aligned with your in-class instruction. Aim to write one comment about this priority area on each paper, using linguistically inclusive commenting strategies. As you think about reapportioning your time, it may helpful to start with some templates to use when you can only write a limited number of comments:

- I understand the thesis of your paper to be . . .
- You do a great job engaging/informing the reader by . . .
- You might better engage/inform the reader by . . .
- I easily followed the flow of your ideas because . . .
- Read your paper out loud to see if it flows the way you want it to.
- Work on moving from just [what the student is doing, e.g., telling, describing, claiming] to [what you want the student to also be doing, e.g., showing, analyzing, synthesizing, citing evidence].

Linguistically inclusive comments can efficiently differentiate instruction. For example, you might notice that one student's paper could benefit from attention to verb tense. Although verb tense may not be a topic you have covered in class, you can use your feedback to provide this particular student with information to make tense more consistent. You can provide a comment or two on this pattern, using linguistically inclusive strategies, such as:

- I noticed a switch from past tense to present tense here. Is that intentional? Think about what tense or tenses you want to use and why.
- I highlighted changes in tense. See if you want to make any corrections or leave it as-is for a particular impact.

If while reading this paper, you also notice a sentence fragment or two that you would typically comment on, don't! Save yourself time and help the student to focus on tense, which you've decided is a priority.

In my study, instructors taught up to five classes a term with up to 25 students per class. When an instructor taught fewer than three classes a term, they had extensive administrative duties. All the same, the instructors made an average of 50 comments per paper, most of which were brief corrections, including crossing out or circling a word. The quick corrections made grading so many papers more manageable. Yet, this approach is rarely the most efficient. Many students are overwhelmed when they see more corrections than they think they can handle. It can also be difficult for students to see where to start. You know what this reality looks like if you've had a student submit a revised paper that looked much the same as the first draft, despite your feedback. When papers are marked with many brief corrections, the aim seems to be a polished paper rather than contributing to the student's writing development. But of course, just as one academic term doesn't allow time for instructors to give all the meaningful feedback they would like, it doesn't allow time for students to learn to produce several polished papers. Rather than attempting to mark as many things as possible that need improvement, instructors can reduce comment quantity to focus on a few priority areas. At the same time, they can increase comment quality by using linguistically inclusive strategies. Fewer, higher quality comments can allow students to develop their writing in ways that are amenable to the time available. The rest of this chapter explains what these comments look like. Chapter 7 goes through more strategies specific to the needs of instructors with extensive teaching loads and no extra time.

USE FEEDBACK AS A CONVERSATION

We want the time and energy we put into our feedback to be worth it. In a linguistically inclusive approach, we want students to engage with and learn from our feedback, whether our goal is for them to develop an individual piece or as writers generally. This approach is how we increase comment quality and effectiveness. Students want feedback to be meaningful too. This topic came up in our student focus groups (see Franz et al., 2022):

> I've been asked [by the instructor] what's going to best help [me] for feedback. That has helped because just seeing, "Oh, I need to change this or that"—how is that making my writing better? Is that something that [the instructor] just want[s] to see?

This student distinguishes their writing development from doing what the professor wants in a given instance. When students have learned to use writing feedback to please an instructor, feedback as a conversation can help them see its purpose in a new, more meaningful way. In response to our *Students' Right to Their Own Writing* guides (srtow.org), students explained that this approach to feedback was new for them:

> When I go to my professor, I approach it from they're going to tell me what I did wrong and I'll fix it. But the [SRTOW] guide turns it more into a conversation about writing and coming into the middle with it instead of me just fixing what they say.

Feedback as a conversation supports metacognition, revision, and student agency. And feedback as a conversation is essential for students' right to their own language. Otherwise, if feedback is one-sided, students learn to assimilate to someone else's expectations ("I'll fix it") without learning how to think about their writing ("How is that making my writing better?"). Even more, when students turn to generative AI like ChatGPT (OpenAI, 2023) to get their writing assignments done, feedback as a conversation will drive them to think critically about the results AI provides.

The rest of this chapter shows what feedback as a conversation looks like from the instructor's end—specific, contextualized comments and questions. To ensure that students follow through with their end of the conversation, you can assign them to respond to your feedback in their revisions, comment replies, conferences, and office hours. Online word processors make it easy for students to reply directly to your comments and to track the version history to see how students revised in response to your feedback. If your feedback is supportive, you can even have them discuss it with each other in peer feedback sessions. When feedback is part of a conversation where students are expected to think critically about your comments, their revisions will be more thoughtful:

> In high school, I remember most feedback was granular about sentence structure and grammar and mechanics. It was a big transition to college when they cared about the broader scope and what you had to say. It was helpful to hear, "Can you go more into this?" or "This seems extraneous." But it took a while to get used to that.

As this student notes, feedback for deeper revisions will be new for many students, especially newer college students. That's why, besides thinking critically about your comments, it's helpful to create assignments where students respond to your comments directly as part of the learning process.

TEACH THROUGH SPECIFIC POSITIVE COMMENTS

Specific, positive comments on language use can help students understand what they're doing well and what valued organization, grammar, and word choice look like. This topic also arose in our student focus groups, such as when we asked students what writing feedback they found most helpful: "Letting me know what I did well; maybe I should continue to do that." Education and composition scholars (e.g., Ball, 1999; Kimball & Jazzar, 2011; Konold et al., 2004) recommend specific positive comments for writing development and honoring students' right to their language.

Many instructors set out to provide positive feedback. Angela, for instance, described wanting to spend her time on what her students do well in their writing (Franz, 2019). Traci Gardner—a writing instructor at Virginia Tech and contributor to the *Bedford/St. Martin's Bits Blog* and the National Council of Teachers of English's *ReadWriteThink* website—similarly explains, "I focus on what I see as the writer's intentions, goals, and strengths (not the weaknesses)" (Gardner, 1998, para. 7). Yet, with limited time and perhaps especially for instructors with large teaching loads, the goal of helping students improve often wins out over a focus on existing strengths. Instructors give positive feedback at a lower rate than constructive feedback, as I found in my study and as previous studies have found (e.g., Biber et al., 2011; Stern & Solomon, 2006). As shown in Figure 4.1, I found a lower rate of positive comments in response to language features, especially word choice, grammar, and mechanics.

When instructors do provide positive comments on a paper's word choice, grammar, or mechanics, these comments tend to be general, such as "free of grammatical errors," "readable," or "clear and smooth writing

Figure 4.1. Percentage of positive and critical comments in response to language patterns

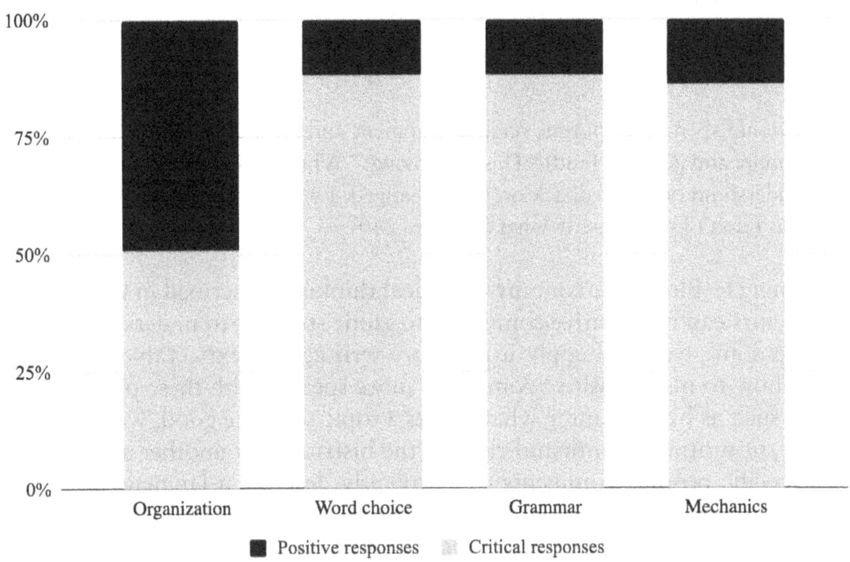

Table 4.2. Make positive comments specific in a linguistically inclusive approach

Traditional Comment	Linguistically Inclusive Comment
No unclear wording that causes the reader to pause	Word choice suits your audience; I can tell who or what pronouns refer to.
Strong word choice	Unexpected word choice captured my attention (would have expected the word *life*).
Good topic sentence	Topic sentence sets up the purpose of the paragraph.
Sophisticated syntax	This stylistic variation between long and short sentences, including fragments like this one, creates an engaging tone.
Clear and smooth writing overall	Your narrative provides a descriptive chronology of events.
Engaging tone	I've highlighted some examples of multiple negation (double negatives) in your paper. I can see that this pattern is part of the voice you are cultivating.
Grammar suits your purpose	Using different grammar patterns like those highlighted suits your message about the power of words.

overall" (see Table 4.2). As demonstrated by a college alum who participated in our focus groups (Franz et al., 2022), general positive comments can leave students wondering what, exactly, was effective about their writing and how to apply those effective features to future assignments:

> I would spend tons of time on an assignment and get a B. Why? Then do it last minute and get an A [and] "This is amazing!" What did I do differently? I didn't understand or get feedback on what changed. I want to repeat what I did here. But I don't know exactly what I did. (p. 240)

Returning to Bloom's taxonomy of critical thinking, described in Chapter 2, instructors can use positive comments to guide students to understand what they're doing well and apply it to future writing contexts. Table 4.2 illustrates how to make positive comments more specific with these purposes in mind, such as by explaining what makes a topic sentence good, word choice strong, or writing smooth and clear to the instructor or another audience.

Specific positive comments can explicitly describe a language pattern, including what the pattern looks like and how it might work in the rhetorical context—with the student's audience, purpose, or voice.

Positive comments aligned with a linguistically inclusive approach may also acknowledge the instructor's subjective viewpoint. In my study, Susan commented on a student's paper: "Unexpected word choice captures attention (would have expected the word *life*)" (Franz, 2019). This comment explains what is good about the word choice (it captures attention) and why (it is unexpected). Moreover, this explanation is situated in how the instructor specifically reacted.

To honor students' right to their own language in writing, scholars recommend teaching language patterns descriptively rather than prescriptively (e.g., Redd & Webb, 2005; Young, 2010). Instructors can apply this advice with sociolinguistically informed descriptions. Whereas prescriptive comments tell students what to do, descriptive comments equip them with information that can help them make their own choices in their writing. The following examples name specific African American English and Southern English language patterns and their positive rhetorical impact:

- I've highlighted some examples of multiple negation (double negatives) in your paper. I can see that this pattern is part of the voice you are cultivating.
- This grammar pattern is an appositive pronoun. Grammar checkers tend to correct it, but it is a legitimate grammar form used in varieties such as African American English. Using different grammar patterns like appositive pronouns suits your message about the power of words.

Following the sociolinguistically informed advice of Young (2010), these comments support grammar as variation rather than grammar correction. Chapters 5 and 6 give information about multiple negation, appositive pronouns, and other patterns that may be useful to name and describe for students.

COMMUNICATE HIGH EXPECTATIONS

The rest of this chapter focuses on strategies for providing more critical feedback. One thing to remember is that it is crucial to give critical feedback in the context of high standards that you believe the student can meet (Cohen et al., 1999). For the sake of time, we often focus on what we think is essential when commenting: what needs to be done to improve the paper. But a list of uncontextualized corrections, though it can seem efficient, might not convey that we think students can develop as writers. A student might read a long list of corrections in particular as an indication that they are a bad writer who can only make edits with specific prompting. Instead, in a linguistically inclusive approach, comments provide information to help students make their own decisions about their edits. Ultimately, comments tied to high expectations will be a better use of time and energy as they give students tools and motivation to develop as writers.

The strategies exemplified in this chapter, such as strategic questions and specific descriptions, imply high expectations. Instructors should also state those expectations explicitly. For instance, experiments by Cohen et al. (1999) found the following comment to be the most motivating for Black college student participants writing a letter to submit for publication:

> It's obvious to me that you've taken your task seriously and I'm going to do likewise by giving you some straightforward, honest feedback . . . you've followed the instructions, listed your teacher's merits, given evidence in support of them. . . . The comments I provide in the following pages are quite critical but I hope helpful. Remember, I wouldn't go to the trouble of giving you this feedback if I didn't think that, based on what I've read in your letter, that you are capable of meeting the higher standard. (p. 1307)

This comment accomplishes the following in line with a linguistically inclusive approach:

- Recognizes the hard work of the student ("you've taken your task seriously")
- Specifically describes what the paper does ("listed your teacher's merits, given evidence in support of them")
- States a desire to help the student writer rather than simply evaluate ("comments . . . are quite critical but I hope helpful")
- Communicates high expectations for the student ("I wouldn't go to the trouble of giving you this feedback if I didn't think that . . . you are capable of meeting the higher standard")

In contrast, students were *not* motivated by the following critiques given without the context of high expectations (Cohen et al., 1999):

> Your letter needs work in several areas before it can be considered for publication. In addition to some routine editorial suggestions that I've offered, most of my comments center on how you could breathe more life into your letter and make the description of your favorite teacher and her [his] merits more vivid, personal, and persuasive. As it stands, your letter is vague and rambling—long on adjectives and short on specific illustrations. You describe your teacher's dedication and commitment but you haven't explained why your teacher is more exemplary in her [his] contribution, more deserving of recognition, than most of the nominees cited by other writers. . . . You need to discuss the long-term imprint [teacher's name] has left on you in greater detail—this enduring impact is perhaps the strongest testimony of a teacher's success. (p. 1306)

Unlike the more effective comment, this comment does not recognize the student's effort or communicate high expectations. This comment describes in detail what the student has not done without much focus on what is already there. Labels like "vague" and "rambling" do not provide helpful information, especially for students who thought their writing met the needed purpose. The rest of the strategies in this chapter provide alternatives to unhelpful labels and corrections. These strategies cover responses to specific areas of a student's paper that can be offered in the context of high expectations.

HIGHLIGHT YOUR SUBJECTIVITY AS A READER AND ACKNOWLEDGE MULTIPLE AUDIENCES

Even while a linguistically inclusive approach aims for specific descriptions of language patterns, this grading approach is not free from subjectivity. Instead, instructors can highlight their subjectivity as readers while they describe and ask about what they notice in a student's paper. In providing students with feedback, Stacey was explicit about her subjectivity through comments such as, "I got a bit lost here . . ." or "I wasn't sure what this meant . . ." (Franz, 2019). In a linguistically inclusive approach, explanations of the instructor's reading experience include explicit reference to the patterns that influenced this experience:

- "I was confused about the garden. It is mentioned several times, but I couldn't understand why it was important" (Gardner, 1998, para. 7).
- I had to read this sentence a few times to understand it . . .
- I noticed a switch from past tense to present tense here. Is that intentional? Think about what tense or tenses you want to use and why.
- I wasn't sure if "you" referred to the reader here. How can you clarify who you're referring to?

Instructors also acknowledge multiple audiences in a linguistically inclusive approach. With few exceptions, the instructor is the students' direct audience in writing classes. Students are writing to the instructor for a grade or other evaluation. Whether an instructor uses contract or more traditional grading, a student who aims to succeed in class will write for the instructor's positive evaluation. At the same time, writing instructors want to teach their students to adapt their writing to multiple audiences. So indirect audiences may be at play in addition to the direct audience of the instructor.

In some cases, an instructor might incorporate an actual external audience into an assignment, such as requiring students to submit their assignment to a university publication or as part of an application. This can certainly give writing the type of meaning students find when they write on social media or when they write for a job and have a real purpose and reader. In many other cases, instructors invoke an external audience in assignment instructions and criteria. For example, Stacey assigned her students to write for their college's students, faculty, and staff for one assignment (Franz, 2019).

Peer feedback also brings in additional audiences; students may directly or indirectly write to their peers when they expect peer feedback as part of the writing process. Finally, even as most students write for the instructor, they may have additional audiences in mind that they would like to write for. Some assignments draw on this goal and ask students to identify their target audience. As part of an assignment or feedback, instructors can pose questions to encourage students to consider who they aim to write to:

- Who would benefit from reading your work?
- Who, whether an individual or a community, is your motivation for writing about this topic in this way?
- As you develop as a writer, who would you like to write to?

All of these audiences—actual or potential—must be acknowledged when instructors comment on students' writing. And they must include racially and linguistically diverse audiences. Acknowledging how students do and can write to this range of audiences supports objectives for rhetorical knowledge:

- Will your intended audience be familiar with this phrase?
- Does it suit your audience's needs to state your purpose up front or to gradually lead them to your purpose?
- The African American English organizational patterns will help you relate to your audience.

In this way, a linguistically inclusive approach regularly emphasizes rhetorical adaptation to audience. This commenting strategy meets goals for rhetorical variation, critical thinking, and real-world writing preparation. Importantly, acknowledging multiple audiences means challenging white and standardized English as defaults in writing. In contrast, traditional critiques related to audience assume a white, standardized-English-speaking reader.

As you consider multiple audiences for your student writers, you'll also want to consider the audiences for your own writing. Who you write to can impact who you teach your students to write to and who you may assume is included in their intended audiences. Who do you write to and for? Why? Do ever you write for primarily Black audiences—if so, when? How do the readers you yourself write to influence the way you address audience for your students? It may be helpful for you and your students to use Black literature across genres as a model for engaging Black readers (Muiru, 2021; Okonkwo, 2021).

ASK STRATEGIC QUESTIONS

In a linguistically inclusive grading approach, instructors pose questions instead of assigning grade penalties when responding to words or structures that seem informal, confusing, or unfamiliar. Strategic questions ask students to think critically about the choices they want to make in their writing without prescribing particular language forms. Strategic questions thus support writing objectives for rhetorical variation and critical thinking. In the following example, the student is asked to think about audience design both in their specific paper and also more generally:

> What are some reasons you may or may not want to use contractions in this paper? Will your audience expect contractions? Can you think of a reason to use contractions even when your audience may not expect them?

These questions engage students at the higher levels of Bloom's taxonomy (see Chapter 2). Students are asked to analyze the relationship between contractions and audience and to evaluate their choices or, if applicable, the ways they use generative AI for writing. These questions imply that the instructor expects students to meet high standards. Point deductions and corrections, meanwhile, engage students in the lower levels of Bloom's taxonomy as students are asked to remember and apply rules.

The following strategic questions can similarly encourage students to consider the impact of word or grammatical choices on their audience:

- I noticed you use "amazing" and "awesome" a lot. How do you think those words will impact your audience?
- What does your use of "I" do to your argument? How might it strengthen it for some audiences? How might it weaken it for some audiences?
- I highlighted generalized words (e.g., "people") and boosters (e.g., "very") that give your paper a conversational tone. How do you think this tone suits your audience and purpose?

Strategic questions can facilitate students' decisions about more global aspects of their writing as well, such as thesis organization:

- How does this section relate to your thesis?
- What do you hope your reader takes away from this question?
- What is your primary purpose? Do you want to state your purpose for your audience or have them infer it?

Gardner (1998) offers a host of adaptable strategic questions and question templates for responding to student drafts:

- "Who is this draft written for? Who is the audience?
- What is this draft about? What is its purpose?
- Where do details and specifics stand out? Where does the text SHOW well?
- Why did you . . .? It's an interesting choice/technique/etc. Why did you choose it?
- How would your draft change if you . . .?" (para. 5)

Gardner's example questions compel students to analyze and evaluate their own writing and, if there is an opportunity for revisions, to create these revisions on their own rather than just apply corrections and prescribed instructions—again communicating high expectations for students. Such questions also support students' linguistic agency as they can determine who they're writing to and why and connect their own language to those goals. Gardner's questions can be adapted to different writing assignment types. For example, "Where do details and specifics stand out?" can be, "Where does evidence support your claims?" or "Where are different sources synthesized?"

CONTEXTUALIZE PRESCRIPTIVE COMMENTS

Prescriptive comments tell students what to do. These comments direct students to edit a feature of their paper without making the edit for the students. The traditional approach examples in Table 4.3 demonstrate what these comments look like. If they provide sufficient detail, prescriptive comments can guide students to revise and may help equalize student access to success in the composition classroom (Delpit, 1988). "Add a sentence that says the paper's purpose" may provide enough information for a student to move forward with that revision. Prescriptive comments with less detail may not be effective in helping a student revise. With "Watch use of apostrophes," students may be unsure of what to do with their apostrophes. With "Clarify *they*," they may not know what is unclear about their use of *they*. With "connect ideas between paragraphs," the student may see their ideas as already connected.

Prescriptive comments that tell students to code-switch from African American English to standardized English have a linguistically reductive and racist function (Young & Young-Rivera, 2013). Comments like "change plurals to the standard form" or "correct subject–verb agreement per standard English" suggest that standardized English is the superior choice without qualification or room for student agency. A linguistically inclusive grading approach looks at code-switching and code-meshing through a racially aware and pluralistic lens, as Young and Young-Rivera (2013) recommend. This racially aware lens means contextualizing prescriptive comments. For

Table 4.3. Rework Prescriptive Comments in a Linguistically Inclusive Approach

Traditional Comment	Linguistically Inclusive Comment	Commenting Strategies Used
Capitalize brand names.	Brand names are typically capitalized.	Specific description
Watch use of apostrophes.	Review apostrophe patterns here: "When to Use an Apostrophe—Quick and Dirty Tips" (Fogarty, 2015).	Contextualizing prescriptive comments
Clarify "they."	I wasn't sure who you were referring to here; make "they" more specific.	Highlighting subjectivity; contextualizing prescriptive comments
I recommend using more interesting and specific descriptive rather than generic words like "amazing," "awesome," and "beautiful."	I noticed that you use "amazing" and "awesome" a lot. How do you think those words will impact your audience?	Highlighting subjectivity; strategic questions
A concluding sentence for a paragraph must be a statement.	What do you hope your reader takes away from this question?	Strategic question
Try to maintain a connection to your thesis and connect ideas between paragraphs.	You imply, rather than state, connections among your ideas.	Specific description
Never refer a reader back to something—always provide the information where it is needed.	I had to search to find the part you were referring to. Maybe restate the info here.	Highlighting subjectivity; contextualizing prescriptive comments
Add a sentence that says the purpose of the paper.	I think it will help your busy readers to state your purpose up front.	Highlighting subjectivity; contextualizing prescriptive comments

example, we can refer to language variation in a way that leaves the decision to the student writer:

> This may a be typo—did you mean *issues*? Or, you may be using variation in plurals. Language varieties like African American English or Southern English sometimes do and sometimes don't use –*s* to indicate plurals.

This comment offers a potential edit—*issue* to *issues*—without suggesting that the standardized version is better. The instructor then describes the language pattern and how it varies. The student can choose what variation to use.

In addition to suggesting a linguistic hierarchy, prescriptive comments can give a false sense of language patterns in academic writing as fixed and nonnegotiable (Baker-Bell, 2017; Balester, 2012; Matsuda, 2006). As shown in Table 4.3, we might comment on a student paper, "A concluding sentence for a paragraph must be a statement." But this isn't always the case and effective paragraphs or pieces can end in a question. We might comment "Never refer the reader back to something—always provide the information where it is needed." But sometimes we might refer to something elsewhere in our work for efficiency (I do so a few times in this book to connect chapters for readers who may read the chapters in different orders to suit their needs.)

When instructors contextualize their prescriptive comments, they maintain space for rhetorical flexibility and critical thinking. This contextualization may be as simple as referring to a resource on the punctuation or mechanics you'd like a student to use: "Review apostrophe patterns here: 'When to Use an Apostrophe—Quick and Dirty Tips'" (Fogarty, 2015). Instructors can also contextualize prescriptive comments by acknowledging their subjectivity as readers—"I had to search to find the part you were referring to. Maybe restate the info here"—or referring to another intended audience: "It will help your busy readers to state your purpose up front."

Contextualizing prescriptive comments can support students' linguistic agency and communicate high expectations by providing them with choices as well as strategies for revisions:

- I highlighted changes in tense. See if you want to make any corrections or leave as it is for a particular impact.
- Try reading this paragraph out loud to see if you want to make any sentence structure changes to help the flow.

In a linguistically inclusive approach, rather than directing comments toward edits that would produce a polished paper, instructors provide comments that will allow the student to improve a few areas of the paper and develop their writing skills for future work. This perspective can be more realistic about common writing processes. Think about your own writing processes, especially for the kind of writing you assign your students. Most of the time, we writers go through countless iterations of a written work before considering it done. Unless students are working on a single writing project throughout a course term, a college class typically does not have the necessary conditions for students to work through a full writing process in this way, so we sometimes compensate by relying on a rubric or telling the students what to do without leaving time for why and how. Yet, students explain that they gain little from uncontextualized instructions:

- I'm used to seeing "refer to the rubric." It's an issue because I [make the change], but I don't know why and probably will make the same mistake again.
- A lot of my professors will leave one sentence at the end of the essay, but if I want to improve, I have to seek that out and figure out specific areas.

Again, many writing instructors cannot afford the time to leave more than one comment per paper, but if these single comments are contextualized, students will take more away from them. When instructors contextualize and limit prescriptive comments to a few priority areas, students can experience a snapshot of this fuller writing process and the work involved to develop as writers—rather than rushing to make a host of uncontextualized edits that, while perhaps resulting in a more polished paper, may not provide any lasting impact on the student's writing development.

RETHINK LABELS

Labels may name a feature of the paper, often an undesired feature, such as "topic shift," "fragment," or "comma splice." Other labels, like "unclear" or "error," evaluate the paper. In a linguistically inclusive grading approach, instructors rethink common uses of labels that may not benefit students' development of rhetorical knowledge, critical thinking, or right to their own language. Labels like "correct/incorrect," "errors," and "misuse" indicate fixed writing standards rather than the rhetorical variation that many writing instructors and curricula aim to teach. Such labels may also discriminate against African American English, Southern English, or other language varieties. Similarly, some labels like "readable/unreadable" and "appropriate/inappropriate" imply a homogeneous audience. In contrast, the strategic questions and specific comments described throughout the beginning of the chapter refer to rhetorical variation across audiences.

Table 4.4 uses a linguistically inclusive approach to rework labels that may be unhelpful or discriminate against students' language—especially labels that refer to correctness, clarity, comprehension, and appropriateness. A linguistically inclusive approach reframes these labels by acknowledging the instructor's subjectivity, asking strategic questions, and providing context and specific descriptions. These strategies give the student writer more helpful information to revise based on their strategic decision-making. In contrast, labels may leave a student writer with a sense that their writing,

Table 4.4. Rework Labels in a Linguistically Inclusive Approach

Traditional Comment	Linguistically Inclusive Comment	Commenting Strategies Used
Formatting to this essay causes challenges with readability	I had trouble following in the places I marked. Reformatting to reduce the extra spaces would help.	Highlighting subjectivity; contextualizing prescriptive comments; rethinking labels ("readability")
Several grammatical problems in this paragraph	Read this paragraph out loud to see if you want to make any sentence structure changes to help the flow.	Contextualizing prescriptive comments; rethinking labels ("problems")
Written in informal tone/voice	I highlighted words that give your paper a conversational tone. How do you think this tone suits your audience and purpose?	Specific description; strategic questions; rethinking labels ("informal")
Paragraph ends abruptly without a concluding sentence	I was left wondering what my take-away should be from this paragraph. Maybe add a wrap-up sentence?	Highlighting subjectivity; contextualizing prescriptive comments; rethinking labels ("abruptly")
Unclear connection to thesis	How does this section relate to your thesis?	Strategic questions; rethinking labels ("unclear")
I do not see a clearly defined thesis	What is your primary purpose? Do you want to state your purpose for your audience or have them infer it?	Strategic questions; rethinking labels ("clearly defined")
An unfocused and disorganized essay	I needed help following your main points. How might you refocus or reorganize to make sure your reader takes away what you want them to?	Highlighting subjectivity; strategic questions; rethinking labels ("unfocused; disorganized")

and perhaps their whole language, is bad, without necessarily providing the tools to improve or learn.

As you rethink labels, it may be helpful to take English professor Catherine Savani's (2021) advice to "Ask yourself what is making the writing unclear to *you*" (para. 15). An important time for an instructor to acknowledge their subjectivity is when they find themselves wanting to label something as "unclear," "unfocused," or "unreadable." Share the burden of communication with your student by describing where you got confused:

- I was left wondering what my takeaway should be from this paragraph. Maybe add a wrap-up sentence.
- I needed some help following in the places I marked. Reformatting to reduce the extra spaces would help.

When instructors want to label something as "unclear" or "informal," they can ask strategic questions. With questions, students have the opportunity to consider whether they would rather make changes to meet your needs as a reader or have other readers or factors in mind that compel them to do otherwise. You can ask questions using the template, "How and why might you challenge or adhere to [academic convention]?"

- How and why might you challenge the notion that argumentative writing is impersonal?
- Why might you adhere to an academic structure for your readers? Why might you challenge it?
- Why might you challenge or adhere to the convention to avoid repetition? Think about your voice and audience.

Note how some of these questions are tied to descriptions of language patterns or descriptions of what made the writing unclear to the instructor. Using such commenting strategies together can help equip students to reflect on your feedback and use that feedback to revise or think critically about their choices in future assignments.

Finally, rather than using labels such as "incorrect" or "grammatical problems," you can instead instruct students to use proofreading strategies or resources that have been discussed in class:

- Try reading this paragraph out loud to see if you want to make any sentence structure changes to help the flow.
- Review *affect* and *effect* here: "Affect Versus Effect—Quick and Dirty Tips" (Fogarty, 2016).

USE CORRECTIONS JUDICIOUSLY

Corrections directly delete, add, or replace a feature of a student's paper (e.g., adding a comma, replacing "accustom" with "accustomed"). Corrections can be a time-saver for the grader—it's often quicker to edit a word or sentence for the student than to explain what to do or direct the student to make choices. Corrections may seem especially efficient for responding to lower-level features, such as grammar and mechanics, which may be why linguistic correction was so prevalent in my dataset. However, frequent linguistic correction, including correction of African American English, does not motivate student learning and can take students' attention away from other elements of their paper (Redd & Webb, 2005). When students work with corrections as feedback, they may apply edits without understanding them, leaving little room for analysis or evaluation. As one college student explained, "When the professor says, 'delete *had*,' I just do it, but I'm not sure why I had to . . . I don't go for follow-up: I just do it" (Franz et al., 2022, p. 240).

Table 4.5. Rework Corrections in a Linguistically Inclusive Approach

Correction	Linguistically Inclusive Comment	Summarizing Linguistically Inclusive Comment	Commenting Strategies Used
issue[s]	Typo? Or plural variation? (Language varieties like African American English and Southern English sometimes do and sometimes don't use *–s* on plurals.)	I highlighted some places that I wasn't sure were typos or language variation. See if you want to make any corrections or leave them as-is for a particular impact.	Specific description; contextualizing prescriptive comments
~~goes~~ went	I noticed a switch from past tense to present tense. Is that intentional? Think about what tense or tenses you want to use and why.	I highlighted changes in tense. See if you want to make any corrections or leave as-is for a particular impact.	Highlighting subjectivity; strategic question; contextualizing prescriptive comments
~~you~~ an addict	I wasn't sure if "you" referred to the reader here. How can you clarify who you're referring to?		Highlighting subjectivity; strategic question
put everything together ~~by nails and hammer~~ [mechanically]	Helpful imagery here		Specific positive comments

Note: Text in *italics* indicates student writing. Strikethrough indicates word/words marked for deletion by the instructor.

As high school English teacher Mrs. Kirsten Bradley has observed, a consequence of linguistic correction is that many students associate revision with correcting grammar and spelling rather than increasing audience impact and fulfilling the writer's purpose (Franz et al., 2022). Although it may seem efficient sometimes, in the end, correction does not efficiently support students' writing development.

In a linguistically inclusive approach, correction is not the default constructive response. Corrections are used judiciously. Instead, instructors can respond with specific descriptions, strategic questions, and contextualized prescriptive comments. Table 4.5 gives examples of how to replace corrections with these linguistically inclusive strategies. Some of the examples of responding to grammar and mechanics also include a summarizing comment. These summarizing comments can be used to respond to repeated patterns rather than comment each time a pattern occurs.

Sometimes even asking the briefest question, such as "typo?" can engage a student with feedback more than correcting what the instructor believes is a typo. By putting a question mark at the end of *typo* when responding to student work, I have learned that what I thought was a typo was in fact a word or phrase I wasn't familiar with.

SELF-ASSESS YOUR PRACTICES

1. About how many comments do you make per paper? Are there ways you could reapportion your time to leave fewer, more focused and meaningful comments?
2. What is the primary goal of your constructive comments? More to get students to move toward a polished paper or more for them to improve in a few areas?
3. What does your own writing process look like? How can your feedback guide students through part of a similar process?
4. How do students engage with your feedback? Do they use your feedback for their revisions? If so, to what extent?
5. Do you incentivize students to engage with your feedback?
6. Do your students know *how* to engage with feedback? How might you help them develop this skill?
7. When do you provide positive feedback? How does your positive feedback support students' writing development? (See Gardner, 1998, for ideas.)
8. Does your positive feedback tend to be general, specific, or both?
9. How do you communicate high expectations for your students' writing? How do you communicate that you believe they can meet your expectations? (See Cohen et al., 1999, for ideas.)

10. To what extent do you focus on what the student is doing with their writing? To what extent do you focus on what the student is *not* doing with their writing?
11. To what extent do you present your comments as your subjective perspective (e.g., in first person)? To what extent do you present your comments as nonnegotiable truths?
12. Who do students write to in your class—both directly and indirectly? How might they have opportunities to write to multiple audiences?
13. When you write, who do you write to? Do you ever write to a primarily Black audience?
14. If you use questions in your feedback, what purpose do they serve?
15. How often do you provide prescriptive comments? What do they look like? (See Table 4.3 for ideas.)
16. What might your prescriptive comments be teaching students about writing and revising? (See Franz et al., 2022, for ideas.)
17. To what extent do you use labels in your feedback? What purpose do they serve? (See Table 4.4 for ideas.)
18. What might the labels you use teach students about writing and revising?
19. How do you respond when a student's writing is confusing to you? (See Savani, 2021, for ideas.)
20. To what extent do you use corrections in your feedback? What purpose do they serve? (See Table 4.5 for ideas.)
21. What might the corrections you use teach students about writing and revision? (See Franz et al., 2022, for ideas.)

LINGUISTICALLY INCLUSIVE PRACTICES

1. Reapportion your time to make fewer, more focused and meaningful comments that students actually address in their revisions or later assignments.
2. Use your comments to guide students through a snapshot of the writing process based on your priorities and the time available.
3. Provide comments that allow the student to improve a few areas of the paper and their writing development—rather than comments aimed at a perfectly polished paper.
4. Use feedback as a conversation rather than to justify a grade.
5. Create an assignment that requires students to reply to your comments. You can use Google Docs or another online word processor where students reply to you directly, or have them reply through their revisions or in office hours.
6. Ask students what they would like feedback on for one assignment. Use their response to focus your feedback.

7. Make positive comments as specific as possible so students learn from them.
8. Use positive comments to describe a language pattern and how that pattern is working rhetorically.
9. Use specific positive comments and strategic questions to encourage students to think critically about the use of generative AI in their writing process and products.
10. Recognize students' hard work.
11. Explicitly describe what a student's paper does in a nonevaluative way.
12. Use comments to communicate your desire to support the student rather than simply evaluate them.
13. Communicate high expectations for your students and associate these high expectations with linguistic agency, not linguistic assimilation.
14. Highlight your subjectivity as a reader in your descriptions and questions.
15. Provide opportunities for students to write to multiple audiences and to choose their audience. Provide feedback that acknowledges multiple audiences.
16. Pose questions that ask students to think critically about the choices they want to make in their writing.
17. Pose questions that compel students to analyze and evaluate their own writing.
18. Provide sufficient detail with prescriptive comments to guide students in their revisions.
19. Contextualize prescriptive comments to maintain space for rhetorical flexibility and critical thinking.
20. Use prescriptive comments to explain how different language patterns work.
21. Rework labels that may be unhelpful or discriminate against students' language. (See Table 4.4.)
22. When a student's writing is confusing to you, describe where you got confused and ask strategic questions.
23. Instruct students to use proofreading strategies or resources that have been discussed in class.

CHAPTER 5

Organization and Word Choice

Writing of all genres benefits from oral and narrative styles. Many Black college student writers effectively employ organizational structures, topic relationships, and word choice rooted in African American English rhetoric—even in their research-based and other nonnarrative writing (Ampadu, 2004; Ball, 1996; Perryman-Clark, 2012). These patterns involve oral traditions and narrative styles that create the engaging reading experience that many of our students are working toward (see Muiru, 2021, and Okonkwo, 2021, for lists of writing that some of our students may wish to emulate). As McMurty (2023) explains, "Black Language is an art" (p. 75). This chapter demonstrates how writing instructors can value and foster African American English rhetorical patterns that engage readers and make writing, even academic writing, appealing.

Because African American English patterns are often rooted in oral forms, a linguistically inclusive approach complicates common notions that students must not write like they talk. As A. Banks (2005) explains:

> The wide body of research in composition that fails to take into account the power of [African and African American] traditions and continues to view Black student writers as less prepared than others, merely "writing like they talk" needs to be questioned and ultimately repudiated as antithetical to both the field's stated goals of fostering inclusion in writing instruction and the actual practice of writers. (p. 71)

When Black college students use oral styles in their writing, they do more than write like they talk: They adapt particular patterns to the flow of their writing, often to compel readers and write in their own voice rather than a formulaic academic one. The same can be true of other students who apply conversational forms to their writing (Aull, 2020). And remember that our students—and most of us—take orality as a starting point when we text, post, and direct message. Many students are adept at this type of writing, and most find joy and meaning in it that they don't find in assigned writing. With linguistically inclusive feedback, instructors guide students to employ conversational forms more consciously to interest and persuade their audience and to find joy in their college writing. This chapter thus offers alternatives to the simplified "writing like they talk" perspective as instructors respond to specific organizational structures, topic relationships, and word choice.

Many scholars have disseminated their invaluable research about African American rhetorical strategies in college student writing (e.g., Ball, 1996; Gilyard & Richardson, 2001; Perryman-Clark, 2012). Such scholars have built on one another's work over the decades. This scholarship analyzes student writing for the use of African American rhetorical strategies such as *circumlocution*, *topic association*, *field dependency*, and *lexical inclusion*, which I describe subsequently. This chapter combines what we know from this body of literature with my findings on how instructors respond to student writing to make practical recommendations for responding to students' organization and topic relationships. As such, I have organized this chapter around the writing features that instructors tend to respond to—*organization*, *topic relationships*, *pronouns*, and *word choice*. My goal is to support instructors in rethinking how they respond to organization and word choice in relation to African American rhetoric. I also encourage readers to refer to the original work of Black composition scholars (Ball, 1996; Gilyard & Richardson, 2001; Perryman-Clark, 2012) for a more student-centered understanding of the rhetorical strategies I discuss here.

As students aim for compelling writing, African American rhetorical patterns can provide a teaching moment for generative AI, whose large-language models tend toward traditional, bland writing patterns (Learn Prompting, 2023). Generative AI can be primed to use more engaging patterns, but this priming takes work (Learn Prompting, 2023). This is especially the case for engaging organizational patterns that are harder to prompt to an AI tool than grammatical patterns. As your students are very likely already using generative AI, you might assign them to take a piece of AI-generated writing and (1) make it more interesting themselves, such as by using the rhetorical patterns described throughout this chapter; or (2) prompt the AI tool to make the writing more interesting in particular ways and evaluate the results.

ORGANIZATION AND TOPIC RELATIONSHIPS

Circumlocution and Topic Association

The orally rooted African American English organizational structures known as circumlocution or topic association are characterized by implied, rather than explicitly stated, claims, topic connections, and transitions (Ball, 1992; Ball & Lardner, 2005; Gilyard & Richardson, 2001; Perryman-Clark, 2013a). Significantly, with circumlocution and topic association, writers do not randomly shift topics but imply connections and themes for the reader to infer. The result is an interactive writing style. As an African American student in a study by Dr. Bonnie Williams-Farrier (2013) described this style, "You just use your mind more when you read it. Cause it's more of like interactive reading, interactive listening" (p. 421). Students don't want what they read to be boring, and they don't want what they write to be boring, either. Our students engage in interactive reading and writing regularly in digital spaces. And the goal to avoid boring writing may be especially important to many Black students whose language and culture incorporate compelling communicative practices.

Mosher (2020) provides an example of a student paper that uses circumlocution to "implicitly [connect] each paragraph to a central focus on the song's effective use of pathos" (p. 443). Following are some transition segments to give a sense of how the student implied these connections and her central theme:

> Nothing seems to engage my mind more than the mysterious world of music [end of opening paragraph]. . . . The emotions that I feel when singing that song are something that I have never, ever felt. Writing this essay even makes me tear up a little / Enough about the emotional toll this song has had on my life though, there is some logos and ethos too [transition from one paragraph to another]. . . . She seems to be drawing the conclusion that when she is gone, people will know she was here. / If I hadn't said enough in the pathos department, I thought I would touch on it again, because the emotion behind the song seems so strong [transition from one paragraph to another]. (pp. 437–439)

As Mosher (2020) explains, the writer gradually takes readers to her thesis as she reflects on her personal experience with the song. The writer shows more often than she tells the import of the song's pathos. She also uses first person to speak directly to the audience—a rhetorical move that is discussed later in this chapter.

Repetition and Recursion

Repetition—of words, phrases, or structures—holds rhetorical power in African American English discourse (see Table 5.1). With repeated words and structures, Black writers and orators recursively structure their work (Ball, 1992). Ball demonstrates how Dr. Martin Luther King, Jr.'s (1965) speech "How Long? Not Long" creates a recursive pattern with a repeated structure around the theme "no wave of racism can stop us": "and the burning of our churches will not deter us; and the bombing of our homes will not dissuade us; and the beating and the killing of our clergymen and young people will not divert us."

When writers, including college student writers, draw on recursion, their written work is imbued with a rhythmic, oral quality. Ampadu (2004)

Table 5.1. African American English Rhetorical Patterns for Organization and Topic Relationships

Rhetorical Pattern	Description	Example
Topic association/ Circumlocution	African American English rhetorical structure characterized by an implied thesis and/or implied claims, topic connections, and transitions (Ball, 1992; Ball & Lardner, 2005; Gilyard & Richardson, 2001; Perryman-Clark, 2013a)	"Nothing seems to engage my mind more than the mysterious world of music [end of opening paragraph]. . . . Enough about the emotional toll this song has had on my life though, there is some logos and ethos too [transition to new paragraph]. . . . If I hadn't said enough in the pathos department, I thought I would touch on it again, because the emotion behind the song seems so strong [transition to a new paragraph]" (Mosher, 2020, pp. 437–439)
Recursion/ Repetition	Repeated words, phrases, or structures for rhetorical effect (Ball, 1992)	"and the burning of our churches will not deter us; and the bombing of our homes will not dissuade us; and the beating and the killing of our clergymen and young people will not divert us" (King, 1965)
Parallelism	Recursion that repeats a syntactic structure (Ampadu, 2004)	"I have fought for my freedom with words, with violence, and with spirit" (Ampadu, 2004, p. 149)
Anaphora	Recursion that repeats the beginning of a phrase (Ampadu, 2004)	"Poetry takes a certain kind of patience to find the right word, the correct symbol, or the right place to pause to construct a work of art that reveals your truth. Poetry relieves me of my stress, exposing my truth and allowing me to take my pain and mold it into something constructive. . . . Poetry opened my eyes to a whole other world, one that gave me a second chance at dealing with life's cruel ways, a world that is now forever cemented, one I can always come back to." (as quoted in Franz et al., 2021)

analyzes examples of college student writers using oratorical repetition patterns like parallelism and anaphora, which contribute to an "elegant writing style" (p. 137). Parallelism repeats a syntactic structure, as in the student example, "I have fought for my freedom with words, with violence, and with spirit" (Ampadu, 2004, p. 149). Anaphora repeats the beginning of a phrase, as in this student example from our *Students' Right to Their Own Writing* website:

> Poetry takes a certain kind of patience to find the right word, the correct symbol, or the right place to pause to construct a work of art that reveals your truth. Poetry relieves me of my stress, exposing my truth and allowing me to take my pain and mold it into something constructive. . . . Poetry opened my eyes to a whole other world, one that gave me a second chance at dealing with life's cruel ways, a world that is now forever cemented, one I can always come back to. (Franz et al., 2021)

The anaphora in this piece contributes to the writer's purpose in discussing his relationship with poetry, a rhythmic genre that tends to draw on recursive patterns. The anaphora also lends an oral quality to the piece, making it likely more captivating for readers.

RESPOND TO ORGANIZATION AND TOPIC RELATIONSHIPS IN A LINGUISTICALLY INCLUSIVE APPROACH

A linguistically inclusive grading approach applies the feedback strategies in Chapters 3 and 4 to encourage students to use a range of organizational structures, including circumlocution and recursion, to draw readers in (see Tables 5.1 and 5.2). Instructors can give specific, positive comments on circumlocution and recursion:

- My interest is captured by the implied connections, which make your writing conversational.
- This type of repetition, anaphora, can give an engaging spoken quality to your writing.
- This repetition recalls the repetition sometimes found in poetry and works well with your topic. It also makes your writing engaging!

Comments like these can be a teaching tool, building awareness of how students connect topics in their writing. A participant in our faculty focus groups explained how they help students find what they value in their writing by positively drawing attention to features, especially nondominant features, of their writing. For instance, the participant may work with a student and say, "Okay, this repetition means something; let's make that more obvious in your writing."

Table 5.2. Responding to Organizational Patterns

Organizational Pattern	Linguistically Inclusive Response	Traditional Response
Circumlocution	What is the main point you expect your reader to infer? What are the pros and cons of leading your reader to that point versus spelling it out?	It lacks focus that would be established with a clearly defined thesis.
Topic association	I can follow the flow of your ideas because of the stated connections. OR I can follow the flow of your ideas because of the implied connections.	Nice transition to ideas—each new idea relates to the previous.
Repetition	This type of repetition is known as anaphora. It gives an engaging spoken quality to your writing.	Three similar sentences in a row—reword for variety.
Prescribed paragraph structures	Closing the paragraph with this citation might take away from your own conclusion.	You cannot begin or end a body paragraph with cited research.
Prescribed essay structures	What context does your reader need to understand the technical information?	This information should have been presented earlier before the technical information was given. You want to think about your audience who are not informed about your topic.

Instructors can also ask strategic questions to help students make choices from a range of organizational patterns:

- What is the main point you expect your reader to infer? What are the pros and cons of leading your reader to that point versus spelling it out?
- What context does your reader need to understand this technical information?
- How does your flow or organization make the writing more or less interactive?

These questions ask students to consider how their audience might read their work, depending on its structure.

When an instructor aims to teach a particular organizational pattern, they can contextualize their prescriptive comments by explaining how the pattern may be helpful:

- Closing the paragraph with this citation might take away from your own conclusion.
- Since your intended audience will probably skim, they will benefit from seeing your thesis up front.

These examples avoid blanketly prescribing a pattern, such as "State your thesis in the introduction" or "Never end a paragraph with cited research." Instead, the student has information to help them make their own decision, and there is space for more than one organizational pattern to be used in academic writing.

Instructors in my study most often prescribed and rewarded organizational patterns very different from the circumlocution and topic-associating structures that link topics implicitly. The patterns consistently rewarded included the following:

- Chronological order
- Formulaic paragraph structures (e.g., topic sentences, one topic per paragraph, concluding sentences)
- A single thesis stated in the introduction
- Explicit connection of each point to the thesis
- Transitions that directly relate points to one another
- A restatement of the thesis in the conclusion

These patterns may be taught in class, or students may be expected to have learned to write with these patterns in prior classes. Like African American English organizational structures, these patterns can be rhetorically effective. Yet, exclusively rewarding these structures can discriminate against Black students who draw on African American English discourse. In addition, when a narrow set of organizational patterns is prescribed, there is little room for the student writer to adapt their writing structures based on their voice, audience, and purpose.

Despite their well-documented rhetorical power, writing instructors tend to penalize circumlocution and recursion. In my study, I found that instructors penalized the following features via rubrics, checklists, and corrections:

- Shifts in topics
- Breaking up topics
- Focusing on multiple points
- Repeated points and phrases

When patterns of circumlocution and recursion are corrected without context, instructors miss the opportunity to teach the rhetorical value of oratorical strategies in writing. Instructors often responded to these patterns with terms like "unclear" and "unfocused." As Chapter 4 explains, such labels can suggest that there is only one way to be clear and focused and that it does not include African American English organizational patterns. Instead, instructors can remember their subjectivity as readers by asking themselves, "What is making the writing unclear to *you*? Why?" (Savani, 2021). Often, our goal is for students to write to various audiences, including their communities. And many readers find the features listed previously more intellectually stimulating than dominant academic patterns (Williams-Farrier, 2013).

Other studies have also found that instructors favor a narrow set of organizational patterns, resulting in discrimination against African American English. Mosher (2020) conducted a study using the student paper quoted earlier in this chapter. The writing instructor participants responded without appreciating the student's circumlocution strategies. They were looking for a prescribed structure with an explicit thesis and criticized needing to infer the thesis as part of the reading process:

- "The student didn't really have a clear thesis . . . It wasn't until I got to almost the end of page two that I figured [the point] out." (Mosher, 2020, p. 441)
- "The first paragraph doesn't even mention pathos at all. And so . . . I mean, I can't surmise that that's what they were talking about." (Mosher, 2020, p. 441)

The student writer did not conform to the participants' expectations for an explicit thesis or theme in the first paragraph, yet the instructors knew the student's main point. Even the reader of the second quotation, who claims to be unable to surmise the theme, determined that the student was writing about pathos. And the student certainly has created an interactive read.

In both my study and Mosher (2020), instructors' rationale for their expectations centered more on conventions—what academic writing is and should be—than on the rhetorical value of voice or the impact on the audience. Of course, an explicit, early thesis can have a desired impact on an audience, depending on that audience and the writer's goals. Such a rationale contextualizes these expectations and provides more information for students' rhetorical development than appeals to academic norms. For example, rather than commenting, "Your first paragraph needs a clear thesis in academic writing," an instructor may comment, "Your reader may stop reading after the first paragraph, so you'll want to have your purpose up front." Frame these rationales for students in variable ways. While an explicit early thesis and other dominant organizational features can effectively communicate the writer's message to their audience in many contexts, so can the implied themes of circumlocution. An instructor can keep this in mind when they suggest specific patterns:

> I can see how you aim to pull in the reader by building up to your point—often, this can be an engaging style. However, the selection committee will likely read many essays at once, so spelling everything out for them is helpful.

While parallel structure is traditionally rewarded in writing classes, other repetition is often corrected. For example, the generative AI writing editor app Grammarly (2023), gives the following warnings:

- "Monotonous sentences: Three or more similar sentences in a row . . ."
- "The word *x* appears repeatedly in this text. Consider using a synonym in its place."
- "X may be redundant."
- "It appears that *x* may be unnecessary in this sentence. Consider removing it."

These Grammarly warnings and similar corrections from instructors overlook the engaging quality of African American English recursive patterns like anaphora.

PRONOUN CHOICE

Pronouns for Lexical Inclusion

Some African American English rhetorical styles use first- and second-person pronouns, including in college writing. These usages serve rhetorical functions. For example, first-person plural (*we*, *us*, *our*) and second-person pronouns (*you*), "inclusive lexical terms" (Ball, 1996, p. 34), allow writers to interact with their audience:

- "Economic inequity is a major problem in America. I am sure *you* have seen this in *your* community." (Franz et al., 2021)
- "*We* must work together to fight against this issue."
- "Everything *you're* feeling right now I've felt, my friend. *You're* not alone." (Franz et al., 2021)

Effective use of lexical inclusion requires an understanding of audience: The student writer must know who they're writing to in order to understand how to effectively include them in the story or argument. Thus, while sometimes instructors may be tempted to instruct students to avoid *we* and *you* because of a potential or actual lack of understanding about audience, student writers' use of *we* and *you* can demonstrate or provide opportunities to deepen rhetorical knowledge. Student writers can also use lexical inclusion as part of their voice. For instance, it may be important for some Black student writers to cultivate a relational voice in their writing.

Pronouns for Narrative Interspersion and Field Dependency

Writers may use first-person singular pronouns (*I, me, my*) to interact with their audience and to personally relate to their topics. With narrative interspersion, writers establish their voices to engage or persuade their readers. While Black student writers are sometimes criticized for narrative interspersion (Mosher, 2020), academic writers well-regarded for their writing style frequently intersperse personal anecdotes in their writing to "humanize the author and give the text an individual flavor" (Sword, 2012, p. 8).

First-person pronouns may also be used to make person-centered arguments, known as field dependency (Perryman-Clark, 2012; Gilyard & Richardson, 2001). Field dependency allows writers to identify with their readers and the topics at hand. Perryman-Clark (2012) provides examples from a student writer in one of her classes:

> "The explosive post brought out anger-fueled AAVE dialogue in the form of reader comments. . . . This takes me back to an observation I made, where emotions play a huge role in the use of AAVE, whether it be happiness, or pure fury." (p. 263)

In this example, the student writer argues from his subjective stance rather than with the more traditional academic distance (Perryman-Clark, 2012). When students are assigned argumentative writing, the topics that Black students find themselves writing about can be close to their lived experiences. As Black students write about policy, culture, and history, their subjectivity can make their writing more meaningful. Field dependency does not mean that a writer excludes outside research. Rather, the writer may be motivated to write about the topic from their lived experiences and can address their experiences from the perspective of existing research or vice versa. The following example is from a student paper synthesizing sources on the concepts of *sounding white* and *sounding Black*:

> I sometimes feel that the way I was raised doesn't make me black enough. I identify with mostly white social groups and I have a white boyfriend. The indicators of one's "blackness," or so to speak, is another thought worth investigating. Due to the fact that language is "linked to racial, ethnic, community, family and individual identity" (Beneke, 2015, p. 129), it is possible that the use of standard English by an African American can be viewed by other African Americans as

undermining the historical ties in which Ebonics, or African American English, are derived.

Throughout the paper, the student writer weaves her own experiences with multiple research sources—strengthening the evidence from both. Removing *I* from the paper would make the student's claims less compelling.

In argumentative and research writing, students may also narrate their research process, including how they reached their conclusions. The use of first person emphasizes the student's agency as a researcher, that they collected, synthesized, and analyzed sources, that they did the work:

- "As *I* analyzed these articles, *I* concluded that . . ."
- "*I* have discovered . . ."
- "*I* decided to use this book in *my* research because . . ."
- "The Conclusion of *My* Research" (heading) (as quoted in Franz et al., 2021)

Academic writers similarly use *I* and *we* to explain how they conducted their research. Authors of peer-reviewed articles use *I* and *we* frequently across many disciplines in the sciences, social sciences, and humanities (Sword, 2012). This finding contrasts with the commonly held assumption that academic writing generally and science writing especially are and should be made impersonal through third-person and passive constructions.

RESPOND TO PRONOUN CHOICE IN A LINGUISTICALLY INCLUSIVE APPROACH

Instructors can respond to pronouns and other word choice to foster students' rhetorical and linguistic awareness. In a linguistically inclusive approach, an instructor might ask students questions or provide them with nonevaluative sociolinguistic information about their word choice (see Table 5.3). Student writers can benefit from the sociolinguistic information given in the preceding sections on how pronouns can function in their writing. In response to inclusive lexical terms, such as *we* or *you*, instructors can explain that the audience is included: "Here, the reader is included as part of the fan base." This nonevaluative description informs the student writer so that they can consider how *we* may or may not be effective in the particular context. Instructors can further explain the differing potential rhetorical impacts of lexical inclusion:

- Including the audience with *we* can draw in your readers.
- Using "you" here may help your readers feel like they're not alone. Or, they may think you're making assumptions about them. Think about who you want your message to reach and how.

Table 5.3. Responding to Word Choice

Word choice	Linguistically inclusive response (without corrections)	Traditional response (including corrections)
First-person singular	How does "I" strengthen or weaken your argument for your audience?	Delete "I" from all academic writing.
First-person plural	Here, the reader is included as part of the fan base.	~~*we*~~ his fans
Second person	Does "you" refer directly to the reader? If not, you can replace it with something more specific.	"I refuse to accept 'you' in an academic essay" (Mosher, 2020, p. 441).
Second person	Using "you" here may help your readers feel like they're not alone. Or, they may think you're making assumptions about them. Think about who you want your message to reach and how.	Avoid use of you in academic writing—makes assumptions about the audience that can offend.
Booster	What is the impact of the word "really" here?	"really" is unnecessary
Booster	How does the phrase "way safer" suit your purpose?	"way safer" is informal language
Phrasal verb	"Going off of" is what's called a phrasal verb. Phrasal verbs make your writing more conversational, which may (or may not) be effective for making your point.	~~*Going off of*~~ *the caption* indicates
Black semantics; Dependent clause	This phrase emphasizes the point following it.	~~*for the simple fact*~~ because *it plays*
Counter; Generalized adverb; African American English and Southern English article ("the") variation	This phrase uses patterns from African American and Southern English and can help engage your readers.	*but* the *majority of the time*
Generalized adverb	Why might you want to (or not want to) reiterate that the following point is your opinion?	Avoid use of obvious wording like "in conclusion, in summary, in my opinion."
Generalized verb	The use of *says* contributes to a conversational tone, so think about whether this is the tone you'd like to strike.	~~*says*~~ claims

Note: Text in *italics* indicates student writing. Strikethrough indicates word or words marked for deletion by the instructor.

Some college instructors contend with students' K–12 experiences as they encourage students to use the first person. In high school, students may have been taught to never use *I* in their writing. In my classes over the years, incoming students have had questions about whether they will be penalized for using the first person in their papers. Some students have even insisted that they should never use *I*, despite my encouragement to the contrary! In this instance, discussing these conventions across writing contexts has been useful. Instructors can share data from *Stylish Academic Writing* (Sword, 2012, see p. 18) that indicates actual first-person use in academic journals by discipline. Sword found first-person pronouns in every peer-reviewed article she surveyed in evolutionary biology and a high proportion of articles from other disciplines, including medicine, computer science, psychology, anthropology, and literary studies. Learning about this variation can help students understand that pronoun choice is more nuanced than blanket do's and don'ts.

While a linguistically inclusive approach aims to foster students' rhetorical and linguistic awareness of pronoun choice, a more traditional approach prescribes pronoun conventions, taking the choice out of word choice. In my study and Mosher (2020), responses to word choice items frequently included the corrections of first-person singular, first-person plural, and second-person pronouns to third-person pronouns:

- Don't put the audience in your story. You are saying the audience is with you.
- Avoid use of *you* in academic writing—makes assumptions about the audience that can offend.
- Is cognizant of the audience and does not use *you* or *I*.
- "I refuse to accept 'you' in an academic essay" (Mosher, 2020, p. 441).
- "The introduction . . . was not critical or distant or some type of third-party objective tone . . . I was looking for that and I didn't see that." (Mosher, 2020, p. 442)

While some of these comments tie pronoun choice and audience, they offer a single view that dictates disconnection from the audience, and, frankly, a more boring writing style. As one of our focus group participants put it, "How do you take into account that students come from different backgrounds and grade them fairly? Students shouldn't be marked down solely because they didn't use the wording of the professor." In contrast, a linguistically inclusive approach embraces the rhetorical effectiveness of connection with the audience through inclusive lexical terms that often make writing more interactive.

FORMAL AND INFORMAL WORD CHOICE

Consider the question—what is formal word choice?—from your own perspective. I encourage you to find a student paper you consider formal and one you consider informal. Highlight the words or phrases that lead you to these assessments: What words and phrases do you describe as formal? What words and phrases do you describe as informal? How do you explain this distinction to students? Aull's (2020) analysis may be helpful for your own analysis. As discussed in Chapter 2, Aull found the following features in students' successful argumentative writing:

- Generalized nouns (e.g., *people*)
- Generalized adverbs (e.g., *our time*)
- Dependent clauses (e.g., clauses starting with *because*)
- Boosters (e.g., *very*, *certainly*)
- Counters (e.g., *but*, *however*)
- Modals (e.g., *could*, *should*)
- Phrasal verbs (e.g., *bring up*, *come from*) (Aull, 2020)

Do you notice any of these word types in the writing you consider informal? You may, as these word types and patterns are associated with conversational writing (Aull, 2020). If not, you may associate other words in your informal example with conversational language. What about the writing you consider formal—are any of the previous word types featured in your formal example? Whether you consider writing formal or informal may depend on the genre assigned. Aull found these conversational features in successful argumentative writing but not in successful explanatory writing, which incorporated more abstract nouns instead. It can be beneficial to determine what specific word types can make writing formal or informal, engaging or boring, in a particular context and to a particular audience. Doing so can provide students with more helpful information than the label *informal* on their writing.

Scholar-educators have noted that Black college writers employ African American English word choice, or what Smitherman calls Black semantics, for rhetorical effect:

- "'Called me a monster' (the best to do it, a winner)" (Hankerson, 2017, p. 37)
- "The most hypest cable television network" (Perryman-Clark, 2012, p. 266)

In a linguistically inclusive approach, instructors attend to the rhetorical function of such idioms and hyperboles from African American English discourse and lexicon. If an instructor is unfamiliar with a student's word choice, such as the phrase "called me a monster," they pose questions rather than negatively evaluate the writing as *too conversational* or *too informal*. Such negative associations privilege some ways of talking over others in racialized ways (Banks, 2005; Hankerson, 2017). Consider Aull's (2020) finding that many conversational word choices contributed to instructors' positive evaluations. Whose effective conversational features may have been excluded? Are African American English patterns based on orality included in positive evaluations? As instructors rework *formal* and *informal* into more nuanced descriptions, they can keep in mind the value of African American English written word choice—and stay open to learning new words and phrases.

RESPOND TO FORMAL AND INFORMAL WORD CHOICE IN A LINGUISTICALLY INCLUSIVE APPROACH

Word choice feedback can present an opportunity for instructors to introduce some of the concepts from Aull (2020) about ways to make writing more or less conversational—another type of rhetorical and linguistic awareness. In the following examples, the instructor provides this sociolinguistic information and leaves it up to the student as to whether or not they'd like to move forward with a conversational tone:

- "Going off of" is a phrasal verb because it takes its meaning from additional words ("off of") that occur with the verb ("going"). Phrasal verbs make your writing more conversational and engaging.
- The use of *says* contributes to a conversational tone, so think about whether this is the tone you'd like to strike.

Instructors can also explain the rhetorical function of African American English or Southern English word choice: "This phrase uses African American and Southern English patterns and can help engage your readers." It can be helpful to provide information about word choice that a student writer may already intuitively know but not be aware of while writing. Linguists refer to this idea as *metalinguistic awareness*. For example, a student may use the African American English phrase *for the simple fact* for emphasis, but, at the time, they may not be wholly mindful of the phrase's purpose. Reminding the student that the phrase emphasizes the point following it can bring students' metalinguistic awareness to the forefront and help them make strategic word choices as they write.

Instructors can provide feedback that directly asks students to consider the rhetorical impact of their word choice (see also the teaching practices of Kirsten Bradley, cited in Franz et al., 2022). In a linguistically inclusive approach, strategic questions can foster students' critical thinking about word choice:

- What might be the impact of the word "really" on your audience?
- How does the phrase "way safer" suit your purpose?

Such questions ask students to stop and consider their word choice from different perspectives and suggest the nuances of word choice that make it about more than formal/informal or appropriate/inappropriate.

Traditional grading approaches tend to negatively label word choice as "informal," "colloquial," or "obvious" without much further description:

- "Way safer" is informal language.
- Avoid use of obvious wording like "in my opinion."
- "Her speech is too colloquial, and she needs to get out of the conversational way in which we speak. . . . We need to move out of that and try to be more formal when we're writing papers" (Mosher, 2020, p. 441)

In these instances, students are told what words to use and, more commonly, those to avoid without the chance to make their own informed choices. There also isn't much attention given to the role of word choice in appealing to readers and avoiding bland writing. Such labels and directives can disregard the rhetorical value of African American English word choice, regardless of the instructor's intent.

In our focus groups, one student described the damaging impacts of racist responses to her writing, especially her word choice and tone:

> When I first got my [prestigious scholarship], my mentor commented on my writing and speech and told me, "Oh, you can't say these words because it's Black English, and it makes you look stupid." She would comment on my notes, "I hope you don't teach this way." In terms of topics, she would nitpick at the topic if it talked about too much diversity, too much race, or my own experience. She would say it was inappropriate. She would comment on the tone of my writing and speech because it was informal. . . . She was a white American, and now I'm more resistant to having a white supervisor. She really doesn't think that I'm able to do my job because she thinks I'm displaying stereotypes of Black people. Even my father has brought up the point that I will always be critiqued. He is critiqued by his colleagues for writing about race and writing. Racism can exist in something that's not living—just by writing things down in a certain way, people are going to judge you. (as quoted in Franz et al., 2022, p. 240)

The mentor harms the student beyond critiquing her word choice; she disparages the student's language, Blackness, and experiences—in effect, the student's whole identity. We can understand how this feedback harmed the student's professional development and mental health. Students' word choice is often tied to their voice, experiences, and the topics they write about. Thus, our responses to their word choice can respond to all of this—and we need to seriously consider the impacts.

SELF-ASSESS YOUR PRACTICES

1. What types of writing styles do your students find engaging? What types do they find boring?
2. Do you ever discuss "writing like you talk" with students? If so, how do you frame these discussions?
3. Do you notice the different ways students use oral styles in their writing? If so, how do you respond to these styles? (See Tables 5.1, 5.2, and 5.3 for guidance.)
4. Do your students use structures such as circumlocution and topic association? If so, in what contexts? How do you respond? (See Williams-Farrier, 2013, for guidance.)
5. Do your students use structures such as repetition and recursion? If so, in what contexts? How do you respond? (See Ampadu, 2004, for guidance.)
6. Do you tend to prescribe and reward particular organizational patterns for your students? Why, and in what contexts? (See Tables 5.1 and 5.2 for guidance.)
7. Do you tend to prescribe and reward explicit or implicit theses and connections for your students? Why, and in what contexts?
8. Do your students use personal pronouns for lexical inclusion? If so, in what contexts? How do you respond? (See Ball, 1996, for guidance.)
9. Do your students use personal pronouns for field dependency and narrative interspersion? If so, in what contexts? How do you respond? (See Perryman-Clark, 2012, for guidance.)
10. Do you distinguish formal and informal word choice in your teaching or grading? If so, how do you explain this distinction to students?
11. What words and phrases would you describe as formal? Why? (See Aull, 2020, for guidance.)
12. What words and phrases would you describe as informal? Why? (See Aull, 2020, for guidance.)
13. How does word choice factor into students' grades or other evaluations, if at all?
14. How do you or can you teach students how to make their writing more or less conversational based on their own goals?

LINGUISTICALLY INCLUSIVE PRACTICES

1. Learn the rhetorical functions of circumlocution, topic association, repetition, and recursion (Table 5.1). Give students specific positive comments describing these rhetorical functions—including making writing compelling—when they use these patterns in their writing.

2. Ask students what writing styles they find engaging and what writing styles they find boring. Then ask how they can make their own writing engaging.
3. Ask students to take an AI-assisted piece of writing and organize it in a more engaging or interactive way.
4. Make space for multiple organizational patterns to be used in academic writing.
5. Ask strategic questions to help students make choices from a variety of organizational patterns.
6. Ask students how their audience might read their writing based on the organizational structure.
7. Reward a range of organizational patterns, recognizing their rhetorical functions.
8. If you want students to use a particular organizational structure, contextualize prescriptive comments by explaining the structure's rhetorical function.
9. Instead of prescribing organizational patterns, present the variation in the structures used in academic writing.
10. Avoid penalizing African American English organizational patterns.
11. When you find a student's writing unclear, ask yourself, "What is making the writing unclear to *you*? Why?" (Savani, 2021).
12. When reading your students' writing, aim to learn new writing styles and phrases.
13. Replace labels like "unclear" and "confusing" with rhetorically based descriptions and questions.
14. Focus on what the student writing *is* doing with their organization and topic relationships, rather than what they are not doing.
15. Learn the rhetorical functions of first and second-person pronouns in writing—including lexical inclusion, field dependency, and narrative interspersion.
16. Provide students with nonevaluative sociolinguistic information about their word choices.
17. Explain the rhetorical function of African American English word choice to build students' metalinguistic awareness.
18. Ask questions and provide information to help students determine whether and how to use first- and second-person pronouns.
19. Explain how first- and second-person pronouns are currently used in academic writing. (see Sword, 2012)
20. Use "conversational" in a nonevaluative way to help students learn how to make their writing more or less conversational depending on their goals.
21. Avoid labels like "inappropriate" that can have racist connotations and harm students and their writing development.
22. Ask students to consider the rhetorical impact of their pronoun and other word choice.

CHAPTER 6

Grammar and Mechanics

When students think of writing feedback, they often think about feedback on grammar and mechanics. Years of emphasis on formal correctness, often exacerbated by standardized tests, lead to this association. In a linguistically inclusive approach, these areas are still important—variation in grammar contributes to students' voice and rhetorical effectiveness. Unlike a traditional focus on grammar and mechanics, though, a linguistically inclusive approach frames grammar as an opportunity for variation rather than an area in which there is a single correct convention.

Chapter 3 asked you to consider and rank your priorities for grading. Based on where grammar and mechanics fall in this ranking for a particular class or assignment, you might decide how much of your attention to devote to these areas. In my research, I've found that even when instructors rank grammar low on their priorities, they still may penalize a student's grade for grammar alone when they determine the paper to be "unreadable." As described in Chapter 3, in a linguistically inclusive approach, instructors read for student meaning and avoid labels like "unreadable." The next time you are tempted to focus on grammar and mechanics in grading an assignment where your goal was to focus on other areas, ask yourself these questions or similar questions:

- What do I think the student is trying to say? And to who?
- Can I grade this paper for (your goal, e.g., analysis, synthesis, evidence) based on my understanding of what the student is trying to say? If not, what do I need to understand to grade this paper?
- Would it help me read and grade if the student first used a grammar checker, such as Grammarly (2023), before (re)submitting the paper to me?

WHAT EXACTLY ARE GRAMMAR AND MECHANICS?

Different instructors define grammar and mechanics differently. Some instructors may prefer to use more specific terms, such as *subject–verb agreement* or *sentence structure*. Word choice can also overlap with grammar.

Some instructors might call the use of *hisself* word choice, whereas others might label it a grammar issue. The line between word choice and grammar is further complicated by the denotations and connotations that underlie particular grammar patterns.

Because of differences across instructors, it's important to consider how you and your students understand terms related to grammar and mechanics, especially when their writing is evaluated on these criteria. These criteria are sometimes tied to audience with the notion that word choice and grammar need to take a standardized form to show respect for the reader, often an implied white reader (Shapiro & Del Russo, 2023; Young et al., 2018). In a linguistically inclusive approach, these choices are instead about considering the wide variations in word choice and grammar that might be relevant to different intended readers. Writing that skillfully engages readers shows a high level of respect for readers—and much writing in African American English does this (McMurty, 2023; Muiru, 2021; Okonwko, 2021).

In addition to framing grammar as variation relevant to readers, a linguistically inclusive approach describes grammar in specific terms that are meaningful for students. If a student gets a high evaluation on grammar and a low evaluation on mechanics, do they know what to focus on and why? Students from our focus group on college writing and Black students' linguistic agency (see Franz et al. 2022) described being confused by rubric and feedback terms that were not explained:

- [The least helpful feedback I received was] "Refer to the rubric." To this day, I don't know what mechanics are. I'm not thinking about that when I'm writing. I don't know what syntax is. I don't know what that means. So I don't know what to do to improve it. In the second draft, it's still there because I don't know what to do if the problems aren't being told to me explicitly.
- I'm told a whole lot, "grammar, grammar, grammar." Why is my grammar bad?

No matter how you define grammar or mechanics for your students, more specific terms and descriptions that point out exactly what you're responding to will be most helpful for them. The obstacle, of course, is that it may not be feasible to take the time to teach students all of the grammar and mechanical patterns that you were expecting, or at least hoping, students would have already learned. A linguistically inclusive approach to grading can help with this challenge. In this chapter, I describe ways to make comments on grammar and mechanics more specific and contextualized.

GRAMMAR PATTERNS

African American English grammar includes patterns not found in other varieties and patterns shared by other varieties, such as negative concord, regularization, and *–s* suffix variation (see Table 6.1). In college student writing, African American English grammar patterns serve various rhetorical purposes. Moreover, African American English grammar has cultural value that is important for students to convey in their writing and reach some of their intended audiences. Many patterns are unique to the language variety and can connote a sense of community with Black readers. In other words, often, students' written grammar is not just theirs but also their community's. This connection makes grammar much more than a surface-level feature in many cases.

A linguistically inclusive approach attends to African American English grammar's semantic, grammatical, cultural, and rhetorical functions. Understanding semantic and grammatical functions can allow instructors to better read for students' meaning and purpose when reading grammar patterns that they, the instructors, may be unfamiliar with. This understanding can reduce unhelpful corrections of student grammar that don't reference larger patterns. Understanding the grammatical and semantic functions of some of their patterns can give students a sense of their options as they write. This sense must be contextualized by the patterns' cultural and rhetorical value, which are more meaningful and accessible than grammatical functions. As one student in our focus group put it, "[Writing development] is not about resembling a certain style, it's more about developing your own style and making it clear for your purposes" (Franz et al., 2022, p. 239).

Grammatically, the African American English double subject or appositive pronoun (see Table 6.1) can restate a complex noun phrase for ease of reading (Rickford & Rickford, 2000), as in the example *The interactions between the kids and the parents, it is relatable. . . .* Semantically, the double subject can highlight or introduce a topic. The first subject can function not only as a subject but also as a heading. In the double-subject version, the noun phrase *the interactions between the kids and the parents* stands out in a way that it would not in a more standardized version: *the interactions between the kids and the parents are relatable.* As an English grammar pattern unique to African American English, the double subject is contextualized in Black culture. Culturally and rhetorically, the double subject is connected to who the writer is and the community they may be writing for.

Meaning Preservation

Table 6.1 demonstrates African American English grammar patterns commonly found in college student writing. Some of the more common patterns that you may have seen in your students' writing are linking

Table 6.1. Grammar Patterns

Grammar pattern	Description	Example
Double subject (Appositive pronoun)	"A pronoun corresponding to the subject noun is inserted after it, creating a second, or double, subject" (Rickford & Rickford, 2000, p. 125; see also Redd & Webb, 2005)	*The interactions between the kids and the parents, it is relatable . . .*
Existential *it*	Variant of existential *there*, which asserts that something or someone exists (Charity Hudley & Mallinson, 2011; Redd & Webb, 2005; Rickford & Rickford, 2000)	*I know that it might be different fun places*
Negative concord	Multiple negatives within a clause (Charity Hudley & Mallinson, 2011; Matarese & Anson, 2010; Perryman-Clark, 2013a; Redd & Webb, 2005; Rickford & Rickford, 2000)	*not really never a dull moment*
Preterit *had* (Innovative *had*)	*Had* plus verb to indicate simple past (Green, 2002; Redd & Webb, 2005)	*However, the inventor had died*
Linking verb (copula) variation	*Is* and *are* may be present, absent, or contractions (Charity Hudley & Mallinson, 2011; Hankerson, 2017; Matarese & Anson, 2010; Redd & Webb, 2005; Rickford & Rickford, 2000)	*It feels like when you done* *I feel like you not free at all*
Regularization	Using regular patterns for otherwise irregular pronouns and verbs (Baker-Bell, 2017; Charity Hudley & Mallinson, 2011; Matarese & Anson, 2010; Redd & Webb, 2005)	*theirself* *programs that is open* *The woods is a place for my artistic side to flourish*
-s suffix variation	*–s* absence on plural nouns, possessive nouns, and third-person singular verbs (Charity Hudley & Mallinson, 2011; Hankerson, 2017; Matarese & Anson, 2010; Perryman-Clark, 2013a; Redd & Webb, 2005; Rickford & Rickford, 2000)	*The advertisement show young women looking at archery target* *gives me way more space than outside do* *someone else house*

verb variation, negative concord, regularization, and *–s* suffix variation; the latter three patterns are also common in Southern English. On the surface, it may seem like such patterns can be simply translated into more standardized forms. So *when you done* would become *when you are done* and *not really never a dull moment* would become *never a dull moment* or *not really a dull moment* when an assignment or instructor calls for standard academic writing. However, a key reason to avoid correction is the meaning change that can result. Both meaning and cultural value can be lost when grammar patterns are changed to standardized versions. *When you done* can emphasize the state of doneness in a way that *when you are done* does not. *Not really never a dull moment* can carry a more understated or even sarcastic tone than *never a dull moment*, and *not really a dull moment* hedges more than it understates. As described throughout this book, a linguistically inclusive approach refrains from traditional corrections.

Many instructors may need to become more familiar with some of the other grammar patterns in Table 6.1. Instructors might encounter double subjects, existential *it,* and preterit *had* in student writing less often than patterns like regularization and negative concord. In turn, such grammar patterns are less likely to be brought up in class than subject–verb agreement, which underpins patterns like regularization and *–s* suffix variation. At the same time, when appositive pronouns, existential *it*, and preterit *had* do appear in student writing, they tend to be salient to instructors. As with the more common grammar patterns, it can be tempting to correct them with a seemingly equivalent form or what the instructor assumes the student means. Yet, these corrections will likely change a student's intent, particularly when the instructor is unfamiliar with the pattern. For example, preterit *had* can be used to indicate a pivotal moment in a narrative. When an instructor corrects *the inventor had died* to *the inventor then died*, the instructor may be missing this meaning of preterit *had*.

Grammatical Function: Making the Most of Word Order

English is a word-order-based language, meaning that more of the language's grammatical meaning comes from the order of words than from suffixes and prefixes added to words. If you know or have learned a language where, for instance, the subject can come either before or after its verb, that language may be more inflection-based—that is, more reliant on suffixes and prefixes than on word order. Although today's English is based on word order, Old English was inflection-based. Many of these inflections were discontinued, but some inflections remain from when word order was more variable. African American English grammar continues to follow this linguistic evolution by varying inflectional suffixes and linking verbs where English word order patterns render them redundant.

A common example of African American English making the most of word order is the language variety's variation in the –*s* suffix at the end of nouns and verbs. In *the advertisement shows*, the –*s* suffix indicates a third-person singular subject (*advertisement*). Word order also indicates that *advertisement* is the subject of the following verb. The African American English version *the advertisement show* relies solely on word order; the suffix is unnecessary. Similarly, *someone else's house* uses both word order and the –*'s* suffix to indicate possession. The African American English *someone else house* uses only word order.

African American English also makes the most of order when varying English's primary linking verb *be*. In most English varieties, the forms *is* or *are* can be fully present or, in some contexts, contracted. Examples of contracted versions are *she's* and *you're*. In African American English, *be* forms that can be contracted can also be absent. So, African American English may use *you are done*, *you're done*, or *you done*. In the latter version, the link between *you* and *done* is indicated solely through word order; the linking verb is unnecessary.

Grammatical Function: Regularization

Making irregular words follow more regular patterns is similarly a common linguistic evolution. African American English grammar regularizes some otherwise irregular verbs and pronouns. Regular past-tense English verbs use –*ed*. Irregular verbs may instead stay the same (like *set* and *cast*) or change a vowel in the past tense (like *take/took* or *sing/sang*). A past-tense form of the standardized English irregular verb *cast* is *cast*. When African American English regularizes *cast*, the past tense is *casted*.

Regularization can go hand-in-hand with relying on word order. The verb *be* is highly irregular with multiple present tense (e.g., *am*, *is*, *are*) and past tense forms (*was*, *were*). African American English makes use of all these forms of *be* and can also reduce these forms to *am*, *is*, and *was*. An example is *programs that is open* or *programs that was open*. As with the –*s* suffix on verbs, the difference in *is* and *are* and the difference in *was* and *were* are differences in the subject of the verb. Again, word order also conveys this information in English, showing, in the previous examples, that *programs* is the subject of *is* or *was*.

African American English can also regularize pronouns. So, the same set of pronouns, the possessive forms—*my*, *her*, *his*, *your*, *their*, *our*—can be used to add the –*self* suffix: *myself*, *herself*, *hisself*, *yourself*, *theirselves*, *ourselves*. In more standardized versions, not all pronouns use these possessive forms; *himself* and *themselves* use the object forms instead, making this an irregular pattern. Note that when combined with –*s* variation in African American English, there can also be *theirself* and *ourself*. *Theirself* may also indicate a gender-neutral singular, called *singular they*.

Cultural Value and Rhetorical Power

In African American English, making the most of word order and regularizing irregular words are about much more than reducing redundant or irregular patterns. Remember that grammar forms are also tied to culture and community. Yes, *hisself* makes an irregular word regular, and *someone else house* gets rid of an extraneous suffix. This framing of grammatical function can help instructors and students see and work with the patterns. But likely more important to the student writer is how these forms are part of their culture and community and, as such, have rhetorical power for their intended audience.

Students in our focus group discussed how African American English grammar was valuable for them as Black writers:

> What would be helpful is getting training in how you maintain your voice across disciplines. That is how bias is manifested. It's not about what I'm saying but how I'm saying it with my Black woman voice. I want to keep my own voice in my writing so that I'm staying true. [It would be helpful for] professors to understand that people will use African American English in a way that is rhetorically powerful but considered incorrect grammar. (Franz et al., 2022, p. 239)

For such students, the issue is not whether they know how to use language patterns other than African American English (they do), but what is lost—Black voice, rhetorical power, community connection—when they do so. Indeed, based on their extensive research and conversations with Black college students across the United States, Charity Hudley, Mallinson, and Bucholtz (2022) explain:

> Language is culture. In the words of some of our student researchers, your language *is* your Black *is* your beautiful. . . . *What* Black people say is a key pathway through which Blackness is transmitted culturally, but just as importantly, *how* Black people talk is a cultural enactment of Blackness in its own right. When we talk about Blackness, we're referring to a broad set of experiences of history, culture, identity, and community. Language is central to all these aspects of Blackness, in all its variability.

We must keep these deep-rooted connections in mind when we respond to student writing, even grammar, in spite of the fact that we are taught that grammar is only "surface level."

RESPOND TO GRAMMAR PATTERNS IN A LINGUISTICALLY INCLUSIVE APPROACH

The linguistically inclusive strategies shared in Chapters 3 and 4 can support students in preserving the grammatical, semantic, cultural, and rhetorical functions of African American English grammar patterns. Instructors can use grammar feedback to bring these functions to students' attention. Nonevaluative descriptions and strategic questions can build students' metalinguistic awareness:

- This African American English grammar pattern is known as preterit *had* or sometimes innovative *had*. It can indicate a pivotal point in a narrative.
- *Obama style* can also be *Obama's style*. This variation works well with your points about style-shifting. Who is your audience? How do they style-shift?
- In African American English, there are different options for phrases like this: *you not free*, *you're not free*, or *you are not free*. In academic English, there is usually only *you are not free*. You can decide which option suits your voice and purpose.
- This is a double subject. Grammar checkers tend to correct it, but it is a legitimate African American English pattern. Double subjects can draw attention to a noun, like a heading. They can also restate complex subjects.

These comments value African American English and provide students with information to make decisions and understand the rhetorical role of grammar. These comments can also make the best use of your and your students' time because they are the type of explanations that AI grammar checkers, which are trained on standardized English, are less likely to give.

More traditional responses, such as corrections, do not provide the instruction students seek. If students are looking or expected to correct typos, spelling, and unintended grammar patterns, they can turn to grammar checkers like Grammarly (2023)—there's no need for instructors to spend their time doing this work! But when students need to understand the rationale for corrections and how their available options might include varieties like African American English, grammar checkers typically fall short. Students in our focus groups shared that if they don't know why they're changing their writing, they will probably make the same mistake. One student explained:

> When the professor says delete *had*, I do it but I'm not sure why I had to. It sounds right in my head, so why am I being told that I'm not correct? This is what my teacher wants to see. I don't go for follow-up because they are the professor and know what they are doing. I just do it. (Franz et al., 2022, p. 240)

This student wants to understand the grammar patterns commented on, but the path of least resistance is following the professor's instructions without seeking deeper understanding. If the student is graded on making this correction in a later draft, there is even less incentive for them to think critically about grammar. This student went on to explain the insight she gained from reading content from the *Students' Right to Their Own Writing* website: "Ooooh, my language style is different from how we're being taught to write." Years of grammar comments and corrections had never framed her writing as different or stylistic, only incorrect and not good enough. Corrections undermine student learning and agency and can change the student's meaning. Deleting an instance of preterit *had,* for instance, can remove the emphasis on the sentence as a pivotal part of the student's narrative.

If you would like students to use or consider particular grammar patterns, they deserve to know what these patterns are and how they work. These explanations can be embedded in both evaluation criteria and student paper feedback. For example, if you would like students to learn about and use third-person singular *–s* on verbs, explain the pattern and why you would like students to use it or at least consider using it:

> "The advertisement show" can also be "The advertisement shows." The *s* at the end is more common in academic writing. Think about which form you want to use based on what you want to get across to your readers.

This comment teaches a grammatical pattern. Students are granted the agency to make a grammatical decision based on their audience and the information they need to do so. This comment is also a good use of an instructor's time because, again, it's not the type of specific explanation that grammar checkers tend to provide but can, in fact, inform students so that they can work critically with the corrections their grammar checkers do provide. In contrast, comments and criteria framed in terms like "subject–verb agreement" hold less meaning for students, especially when the verb in a phrase like *the advertisement show* does in fact agree with the subject in African American English. An explanation in this instructor comment has advantages over simply telling the student what to do, as in, "use third-person singular *–s*." While this prescribed grammar pattern gives more information than a comment like "subject–verb agreement error," it does not help the student understand how third-person singular *–s* operates, nor does it grant students the right to their own language. More general concepts, like "standard syntax" or "correct grammar," have even less meaning for many student writers. These more general terms especially confuse students whose grammar is corrected when "it sounds right in [their] head" or sounds right to their intended readers.

Another commenting strategy for grammar in a linguistically inclusive approach is asking strategic questions, which allows instructors to read for student meaning and to give the student agency. Questions can help instructors avoid assuming whether something was a mistake. For instance, if a student writes *Obama style*, that could be *–s* variation or a typo. It is more beneficial to ask rather than assume what's behind the feature. Such clarifying questions can be asked succinctly: "Can also be *Obama's style.*

Intentional or a typo?" Notably, the question is contextualized with a brief explanation of the variation.

Incorrect assumptions can confuse student writers and discourage them from using and developing their own voices. Hankerson (2017) provides a close-up look at how writing instructor comments thus impacted the relationship Aaron, a Black college student, had with writing. Hankerson and Aaron analyzed instructor responses to an essay of Aaron's; the assignment criteria mentioned both voice and academic language. Aaron, "no matter how hard [he] tried" (p. 35), received negative feedback on both criteria. His grammar and word choice were corrected when he used his own voice. An example is Aaron's use of the double subject in *The guys they helped me*, to which the instructor responded by striking through *they*. Aaron's instructor also marked his grammar patterns as "casual" (p. 37). Yet, when Aaron worked to write with academic language, his grammar was labeled "confusing" and "unclear" (p. 37). In these instances, Aaron used a dictionary to sound academic because his own voice had been corrected, despite "voice" being a graded criterion. As a student in our focus group put it, "The professor said I want to hear your own voice and I was like, 'What did that even mean?'" (see Chapter 3 and Purdue OWL, 2022, for ideas on responding to this question). Without the support to develop either his own voice or conventional academic writing, Aaron withdrew from the class. He retook the course later with Hankerson. In contrast to his previous writing instructor, Hankerson's pedagogy aligns with a linguistically inclusive and Black-centered approach, and Aaron was more successful in this class. She recommends that instructors work with students to understand their voice and learn and sustain students' African American English writing patterns to prevent incorrect and harmful assumptions.

An essay in the *Chronicle of Higher Education* (Smith, 2023) reveals the assumptions underlying the unhelpful approach that Aaron encountered in his original writing course. The author describes student writers from a deficit perspective:

> The worst struggled with grammar—subject–verb agreement, consistency of tense, etc.—but for the majority the problem was style. The students seemed to have all learned together a stilted, awkward, and at times painfully florid way of writing removed both from the rhythms of good prose and ordinary conversational English. It was the voice of someone who wanted very much to seem smart but did not yet know how to do so. (para 3)

This stance is counter to a linguistically inclusive approach. First, Smith assumes that variation in subject–verb agreement and tense consistency indicates struggling with grammar. Yet, for speakers of African American English or other varieties, this variation is part of their language, not due to linguistic difficulty. Second, Smith fails to see the connection between these grammar and style patterns. Yet, for Aaron and many other students, the incorrect assumptions about their grammar are what lead to "stilted, awkward" structures. If a student's "ordinary conversational English" is routinely corrected or penalized, then it makes sense that they would work to remove their conversational language, their voice as Hankerson describes it, from their class papers. Aaron wasn't trying to "seem smart" but trying to meet the instructor's expectations when his own voice wasn't accepted.

Therefore, a linguistically inclusive grading approach avoids using labels that are likely unhelpful for students, such as "confusing" or "incorrect." A comment like "confusing sentence structure" does not indicate what is confusing about the sentence structure, which was likely clear to the student writer. In a linguistically inclusive approach, instructors share the burden of communication (Lippi-Green, 2012), familiarizing themselves with the written grammar patterns of their students, asking questions, and showing their work to understand student meaning:

> I read this sentence a few times to understand what was relatable. Maybe reword? Or your intended audience may be more familiar with this sentence structure. Could get peer feedback on this.

A linguistically inclusive approach also rethinks labels of formality and academic or disciplinary appropriateness. It's essential to keep in mind that limiting what counts as "academic," "college-level," and "formal" often means gatekeeping and devaluing African American English and Southern English. Instead, writing instructors can use their positions to expand what it means for writing to be academic, appropriate, or scientific. Moreover, feedback can be used for students to develop their metalinguistic awareness to evaluate current conventions:

> Traditional academic convention excludes double negatives. How and why might you challenge this convention or stick to it for your readers or your voice?

This comment provides the traditional convention, and framing it as a choice rather than doctrine encourages the student to think critically about whether to use it. A more traditional comment, "Double negative—Your readers will expect a more academic voice," devalues the African American English pattern and delimits the audience and the student's academic voice for the student—preventing the student's critical thinking on these points. Nonevaluative descriptions and strategic questions are used instead to validate students' voices and develop their metalinguistic and rhetorical awareness of grammar patterns.

A linguistically inclusive grading approach does not penalize African American English grammar patterns, avoiding grading bias. A helpful rule of thumb is to resort to questions when unsure of a student's meaning or unfamiliar with their sentence structure. If you truly feel compelled to grade on standardized grammar forms, limit the patterns you grade and teach them explicitly and nonevaluatively. For example, contextualize prescriptive comments, as recommended in Chapter 4, so that standardized English patterns are not treated as superior.

MECHANICAL FEATURES

Mechanical features include punctuation, letter case, spelling, typos, and format, such as spacing, indenting, and font. In my study, mechanical features were responded to by instructors more often than grammar, word choice, organization, and content. Fifty-one percent of the comments in the whole dataset referred to mechanics, and 39% of all the comments on language referred to mechanics (see Figure 6.1). This proportion of comments is particularly notable as mechanics are often low on instructors' teaching and even grading priority list. So, in my study, mechanics did not greatly impact students' grades, even though half of all comments students received were in response to mechanical features. In this case, a student might see

Figure 6.1. Responses to language patterns by type

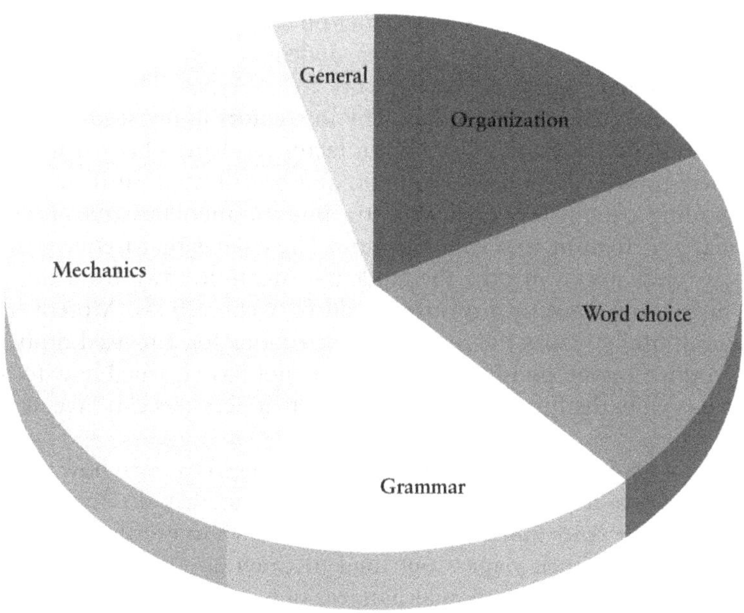

their paper full of punctuation and spelling corrections yet receive a grade mainly based on other aspects, such as analysis and organization. This discrepancy can confuse students and inadvertently lead them to think that high grades and the revision process are primarily based on mechanical correctness when they are not (see also Redd & Webb, 2005). Such implicit messages emphasize assimilation over students' linguistic agency.

Not all students encounter this discrepancy in feedback on their college writing. Some, including those in our focus group, are surprised to find a focus on content when they get to college: "In high school, I remember most feedback was granular about sentence structure and grammar, and mechanics. It was a big transition to college when they cared about the broader scope and what you had to say."

Mrs. Bradley, a high school teacher in one of our focus groups (Franz et al., 2022), discussed her incoming seniors' perception that writing is about correcting surface-level features. She tries to expand this perception by, for example, asking students to share the impact of their peers' writing on them as readers. Such a shift from correctness to rhetoric aligns with many instructors' course goals for critical thinking and rhetorical awareness. It's also important to note that correcting mechanics is not the most efficient use of our time—we can encourage students to use a grammar checker instead so that we can focus our time on more linguistically inclusive feedback.

Proofreading and Typos

While our primary objectives may center on critical thinking and rhetorical awareness, we still want to teach our students to proofread and support them in producing polished written work free of typos. These primary and secondary objectives likely explain why instructors in my study responded so frequently to mechanics but did not factor mechanics heavily into grading. They prioritized purpose, content, and organization in their teaching and grading criteria yet took the extra time to annotate students' typos, spelling, punctuation, and capitalization. The issue is that frequent corrections to mechanics can take the student's attention away from the areas that instructors want to prioritize (Redd & Webb, 2005). Moreover, if a student dutifully makes the instructed corrections for a revised draft, they will produce a more polished piece but may not have learned how to do so on their own in the future. And again, grammar checkers can save us much of this effort.

Even with grammar checkers, students will need to learn how to proofread themselves to make sure that any corrections they do or don't make align with their voice and intention. Teach students to proofread by requiring them to read their papers out loud to catch any typos or other mistakes. If you've noticed particular patterns of typos—say, missing words or spelling mistakes—you can instruct students to focus on those patterns. If you include peer editing in your classes, reading aloud can be incorporated there, with paired students reading all or a portion of their paper out loud to each other. Or, students can be required to write a memo with the name of someone they read their paper to and what changes they made as a result. In this way, students can make changes or corrections based on how *they* want their work to sound rather than the instructor's vision. Suppose you aim to prioritize purpose, content, and organization. In that case, students' proofreading should follow those efforts so that those priorities are not overlooked in favor of mechanical correctness. Remember that many high school and college students have learned to focus on mechanical correctness, so it's useful to be deliberate in shifting their focus to other areas.

A linguistically inclusive approach does not refrain altogether from comments on typos. In a linguistically inclusive approach, instructors guide students to proofread their own work but also recognize that even the most experienced writers often overlook their typos and benefit from others' proofreading. In a linguistically inclusive approach, an instructor is more likely to pose a question than to make a correction for the student. Simply asking, "typo?" gives the student linguistic agency and makes the student an active participant, rather than passively applying a correction. In response to "typo?" on her paper, one of my students explained that the word variation she was using was common in her discipline—something I was previously unaware of. If I had simply made the correction I assumed was necessary, we both may have missed an opportunity. I reiterated my explicit approach to feedback as a conversation throughout the course, which probably also contributed to the student's response.

Spelling and African American English

In writing, pronunciation variation can be realized as spelling variation. Consonant cluster pronunciation and spelling provide a common example. So, the word *guest* may be pronounced with a single final consonant (*gues*) in the speech of many English speakers. Compared to other English varieties, there is a broader variation in pronouncing consonant clusters in African American English, where *guests* may also be pronounced as *gues*. Most college students will not vary their spelling of *guest* or *guests*, or similar types of suffixes, in class writing. However, where there does tend to be spelling variation based on consonant clusters is in *–ed* suffixes.

With consonant cluster variation, *accustomed* and *gossiped* may be pronounced as *accustom* and *gossip*. These examples have more factors than the *guest* example: The spellings *accustom* and *gossip* are standardized forms—just for the present tense and not the past. So you may be more likely to find spelling variation in past-tense forms in your students' writing than in some other consonant clusters.

Variation in *–ed* can be tricky to respond to because the suffix has a grammatical function besides being part of a consonant cluster. Instructors thus might respond with comments like "make tense consistent" or "use past tense." If the pattern reflects spelling variation, though, these comments will not be constructive for the student, especially in their future writing. The key is to avoid assuming what the pattern is about. *Accustom* when you're expecting *accustomed* can be spelling variation, tense variation, or an uncorrected typo. And a grammar checker may not get it right. Depending on the class context and your individual approach, you may reply with a simple "typo?" Make sure to frame this question for students in class as an actual question and not a correction so that they understand that "No, this is intentional, not a typo" will be an accepted response. If you have more room and time, you may want to provide more context:

> Do you want to write *accustomed* here for a past-tense spelling? Standardized English uses the *–ed* for past tense, but not every language variety does.

At first, this comment may not seem too different from "be consistent with past tense." However, this comment refers to both tense and spelling and thus is more adaptable to whether the student intended present tense, past tense without *–ed,* or past tense with *–ed* (typo). Asking a question avoids assuming that the student intended present tense—the assumption underlying comments like "be consistent with past tense."

SELF-ASSESS YOUR PRACTICES

1. What do your students believe about the role of grammar and mechanics in their writing and writing in general?
2. How do you define grammar and mechanics? How do you define these terms for your students?
3. How much time and energy would you like to spend on grammar and mechanics for your students? Why? Can any of this time and energy be off-loaded to a grammar checker, like Grammarly (2023)?
4. How do grammar and mechanics influence students' grades in your class? What is your rationale, or, what changes can you make?
5. How do audience considerations interact with your approach to grammar?
6. How do your students know what to focus on as a result of your evaluation of their grammar or mechanics?
7. How do you typically respond to grammar and mechanics in student papers, if at all?
8. What grammatical and mechanical patterns do you notice in your students' writing? (See Table 6.1 for guidance.)

9. How much of their grade do your students believe is influenced by grammar or mechanics? Does their belief match your intention?
10. Do your students receive any mixed messages—from your class or elsewhere—about using their own voice and academic convention? How might you mitigate these mixed messages and help students cultivate their voices if so? (See Hankerson, 2017, for ideas.)
11. How can your class be a place where student writers can expand what it means for writing to be academic, appropriate, or scientific?

LINGUISTICALLY INCLUSIVE PRACTICES

1. Define grammar, mechanics, and related terms for students and describe how they will be evaluated, if at all, on these areas.
2. When you want to prioritize other criteria over grammar and mechanics, ask yourself the following:
   - What do I think the student is trying to say?
   - Can I grade this paper for [your goal, e.g., analysis, synthesis, evidence] based on my understanding of what the student is trying to say? If not, what do I need to understand to grade this paper?
   - Would it help me read and grade if the student first used a grammar checker, such as Grammarly (2023), before (re)submitting the paper to me?
3. Use Table 6.1 to learn about African American English grammar patterns common in college student writing. Avoid penalizing students for these patterns.
4. Focus on African American English's grammatical, semantic, cultural, and rhetorical functions.
5. Before correcting a student's grammar, ask yourself the following:
   - Might this correction change the student's meaning?
   - Does word order render the correction unnecessary?
   - Does the student's grammar regularize an irregular grammatical form?
   - How might the grammar help the student reach their audience?
   - How might the grammar carry cultural or rhetorical power?
6. Use nonevaluative descriptions instead of corrections to build students' metalinguistic awareness.
7. Ask strategic questions when unsure of a student's meaning or unfamiliar with their sentence structure.
8. Give students the agency to make grammatical decisions and the information they need to do so.
9. Replace unhelpful labels with specific explanations.

10. If you truly feel compelled to grade on standardized grammar forms, limit the patterns you grade and teach them explicitly and nonevaluatively so that you are supplementing, rather than repeating, the work of grammar checkers.
11. Encourage students to determine and work with their readers' expectations independently—rather than telling students what these expectations are.
12. Ask students to share the impact of their peers' writing on them as readers.
13. Have students read their papers out loud to catch any typos or other mistakes.
14. If you aim to prioritize purpose, content, and organization, proofreading should come after those efforts so that your priorities are not overlooked in favor of mechanical correctness.
15. Ask, instead of asserting, "typo?"
16. When commenting on tense, consider that spelling variation may be what's actually at play.

CHAPTER 7

Putting It All Together

A linguistically inclusive grading approach honors students' right to their own language and Black linguistic justice, guides students in making rhetorical choices, and facilitates students' use of feedback. In these ways, a linguistically inclusive approach maximizes the high impact of writing courses for all students.

Writing-intensive courses are considered a high-impact practice—a pedagogical practice found to support college student success at high rates (Kuh, 2008). Other evidence-based, high-impact practices include undergraduate research, community-based learning, and first-year seminars. High-impact practices have been found especially beneficial for students from backgrounds underrepresented in higher education. As discussed in Chapter 1, writing-intensive courses have a high impact when students learn to write with different forms for different audiences (Kuh, 2008). Many writing-intensive courses make rhetorical variation an explicit learning goal. A linguistically inclusive grading approach is necessary to fully support these goals and, in turn, ensure that writing-intensive courses function as a high-impact practice, including for Black college students.

Despite setting goals for rhetorical variation, instructors often assess student writing based on a singular form of writing and a narrow audience, sometimes based on who instructors actively write for or who they were taught to write for (Franz, 2019; Franz et al., 2022; Mosher, 2020). Seemingly conflicting objectives for academic appropriateness and conventions win out over objectives for rhetorical variation. In these contexts, the audience that writing assessment is based on tends to be explicitly "academic" and implicitly white. To succeed, students must restrict their writing's content and form to white modes of knowing and expression. When students lack the opportunity to vary their writing and intended readers, a writing intensive course no longer has a high educational impact. It can even be detrimental for Black and other students. Conversely, when instructors adopt an equity pedagogy (J. Banks, 2020), such as in a linguistically inclusive approach, they can ensure that writing-intensive courses have a high impact for *all* students.

A LINGUISTICALLY INCLUSIVE APPROACH TO GRADING: SUMMARIZED

A linguistically inclusive grading approach not only supports more students in successful writing development but also reframes what that success looks like. For example, in a linguistically inclusive approach, Black students do not have to sacrifice their Black voices or identities to succeed. This book opened with questions about your grading process, including what you look for and why. In a linguistically inclusive grading approach, an instructor will look for how students can do the following:

- Know who they are writing to and for and why
- For Black students, "develop their Black voices as an academic convention" (Richardson, 2003, p. 138)
- Meet their own goals for writing
- Demonstrate linguistic agency and linguistic flexibility

We can also examine how we use feedback to support students in these goals. This way, we can look at our feedback as an integral part of our teaching so that we can make the most effective use of that feedback, both formative and summative. In a linguistically inclusive approach, here's how instructors use feedback to support student writing:

- Validate and foster the language of Black students
    - » Communicate high expectations inclusive of African American English (Chapters 4 and 5)
    - » Give feedback that describes the value of African American English (Chapters 5 and 6)
    - » Develop metacognition by providing descriptive comments that tie students' language use to their purpose and multiple audiences (Chapters 4, 5, and 6)
    - » Attend to the semantic, grammatical, cultural, and rhetorical functions of African American English grammar (Chapter 6)
- Reward linguistic flexibility rather than linguistic assimilation
    - » Show students how they are developing their voice and style with nonevaluative description (Chapter 4)
    - » Acknowledge multiple audiences (Chapter 4)
    - » Ask students to share the impact of their peers' writing on them as readers (Chapter 3)
    - » Give students the agency to make linguistic decisions and the information they need to do so (Chapters 5 and 6)
    - » Have students read their papers out loud (Chapters 3 and 6)

   - Use corrections judiciously (Chapter 4)
   - Avoid penalizing African American English patterns (Chapter 3)
- Use feedback as a conversation
   - Read for student meaning rather than to penalize (Chapter 3)
   - Ask questions to help students make their own linguistic choices (Chapter 4)
   - Ask questions to help students understand how standards are constructed and reconstructed (Chapters 4, 5, and 6)
   - Highlight the instructor's subjectivity as a reader (Chapter 4)
   - Maximize multiple drafts (Chapter 3)
- Use and explain sociolinguistically informed grading criteria
   - Refer to rhetorical variation (Chapter 2)
   - Align teaching, feedback, and grading (Chapters 2 and 3)
   - Teach through specific positive comments (Chapter 4)
   - Contextualize prescriptive comments (Chapter 4)
   - Rework terms like *formal* and *informal* into more nuanced descriptions (Chapter 5)

These strategies can help us rethink not only how we assign good grades but also whether and how we assign failing grades. A linguistically inclusive approach recognizes that failing grades can limit students' learning and educational opportunities (Coleman et al., 2016; Hankerson, 2017; Perryman-Clark, 2016; Sonnenmoser, 2009). Students who may be struggling with a writing class will learn more from supportive, sociolinguistically informed feedback than from failing or retaking the class and receiving the same punitive assessment (see Hankerson, 2017). Such students often have "the most to lose by being told once again . . . that they are poor/bad/struggling/remedial/basic writers" (Helmbrecht, 2007, p. 306).

While implementing the strategies of a linguistically inclusive approach, instructors understand the rhetorical function of African American English writing patterns such as the following:

- Circumlocution—a rhetorical style with implied, rather than explicitly stated, claims, topic connections, and transitions
- Recursion—repetition of words, phrases, or structures
- Lexical inclusion—first-person plural (*we*, *us*, *our*) and second-person pronouns (*you*) that allow writers to interact with their audience
- Narrative interspersion—first-person narratives interspersed in nonnarrative writing
- Field dependency—person-centered arguments
- Double subject—two consecutive subjects usually with the first subjective a noun and the second a pronoun
- Existential *it*—"it is" as a variant of "there is"
- Negative concord—multiple negatives within a clause

- Preterit *had*—"had" before a verb to indicate the simple past tense, often indicating a pivotal point in a narrative
- Linking verb variation—"is" and "are" may be present, absent, or contractions
- Regularization—shifting irregular pronouns and verbs to regular patterns
- *–s* suffix variation—the *–s* suffix may be present or absent on plural nouns, possessive nouns, and singular third-person verbs
- Spelling variation—spelling variation based on pronunciation variation

Chapters 5 and 6 provide examples and further explanations of these patterns.

APPLICATION OF MULTICULTURAL EDUCATION AND CULTURALLY SUSTAINING PEDAGOGY

Linguistically inclusive feedback strategies practically apply multicultural education and culturally sustaining pedagogy tenets. The strategies of a linguistically inclusive grading approach enact J. Banks's (2020) dimensions of multicultural education, including equity pedagogy, transformation and social action curricula, knowledge construction, and prejudice reduction. Rewarding linguistic flexibility instead of linguistic assimilation is essential for an equity pedagogy. To facilitate the success of all students, instructors need to recognize the linguistic practices of all students for their rhetorical potential. A linguistically inclusive grading approach also aligns with Banks's transformation and social action approaches to curricular content, where the goals are to transform biased curricula and to take action against discriminatory policies and practices. Many strategies in a linguistically inclusive approach oppose racist grading policies and practices. For example, when instructors attend to African American English patterns' semantic, grammatical, cultural, and rhetorical functions, they counter grading that eliminates linguistic differences. When instructors grade with high expectations, inclusive of African American English, they counter grade deflation (Agnew, 1997).

A linguistically inclusive approach draws instructors' and students' attention to knowledge construction (J. Banks, 2020)—specifically, how standards are constructed and reconstructed. Instructor comments are aimed at who gets to decide how students write, rather than just the what, why, and how of conventions. Instructors moreover avoid assuming a standard language ideology by describing the positive functions of African American English, reading for student meaning, and acknowledging multiple audiences. Finally, a linguistically inclusive approach reduces prejudice in response to student writing. Common descriptors that can be biased, such as *inappropriate*, *confusing*, *incorrect*, or *informal*, are replaced with more nuanced descriptions that tie students' language to their purpose and multiple audiences.

A linguistically inclusive approach helps instructors enact culturally sustaining pedagogy in writing instruction. As Alim and Paris (2017) explain, culturally sustaining pedagogy "sees the outcome of learning as additive rather than subtractive" (p. 1); this is the outcome in code-meshing pedagogy as well (Young et al., 2018). Responding to student writing with a linguistically inclusive approach expands the possibilities of writing for students while holding students' existing language practices as part of excellent writing. Specific strategies that support additive learning are describing the positive functions of African American English, developing metacognition, referring to rhetorical variation, showing students how they are developing their voice, and asking questions to help students make their own linguistic choices. In contrast, more traditional responses can contribute to subtractive learning; corrections, labels, and fixed conventions reduce rather than expand students' linguistic repertoires.

Culturally sustaining pedagogy aims to "perpetuate[s] and foster[s] . . . linguistic, literate, and cultural pluralism" (Alim & Paris, 2016, p. 1). In a linguistically inclusive grading approach, instructors perpetuate linguistic pluralism when they refer to rhetorical variation, highlight their subjectivity, and tie students' language use to their purpose and multiple audiences, among other strategies. With these strategies, instructors frame writing as variable—not as correct.

WHAT CAN A LINGUISTICALLY INCLUSIVE GRADING APPROACH LOOK LIKE IN *YOUR* CLASSROOM?

College writing classrooms look different across schools, departments, and individual instructors. There may be a host of factors influencing the approaches you use in your classroom. The number, size, and format of your classes can play a big role. Other factors may include departmental policies, your individual teaching philosophy, and your students' language practices and previous writing experiences. The good news is that you can adapt a linguistically inclusive approach to your context as long as you give feedback on students' writing. Here, I address questions instructors may have about a linguistically inclusive grading approach based on everyday writing class contexts.

If you have a large teaching load, which may be the case for most writing instructors, you probably don't have time to ask all the questions and provide all the specific descriptions you'd like on each student's paper. You can still use this approach! Start by setting up your curriculum, instruction, and grading criteria for a linguistically inclusive approach. Center your course goals on rhetorical knowledge and critical thinking. If your course goals include conventions and appropriateness, frame these goals so that students can determine what language features are appropriate. Use the time and space you *do* have: the classroom. Teaching strategies that you may be able to incorporate include the following:

- As part of class lessons, develop students' metacognition by drawing their attention to how and why they and other writers make decisions about their writing.
- In class or for homework, have students analyze and evaluate the organizational structures of course readings. Use these evaluations to teach students to vary organizational styles rhetorically.
- Ask students in class or for homework to find examples of African American English in formal letters or academic writing.
- If you teach peer feedback sessions, have students read their papers out loud to each other. Another strategy is to have students describe their peer's paper's impact.
- Ask students who they want to reach with their writing. Discuss real-world audiences and include Black readers and African American English speakers in the audiences that students write to.
- In class and other communication with students, describe language using terms such as variation, patterns, styles, options, language variety, African American English, and Southern English.
- Teach the organizational, grammatical, or other strategies you expect students to use in their papers.
- Use sociolinguistically informed grading criteria, and explain its importance in class.

Next, take stock of your current grading practices, particularly the time you spend on grading. How much time do you devote to each paper? How are you spending this time? In a traditional grading model, even writing instructors with large teaching loads sometimes comment heavily on student papers. In my study, instructor participants prioritized feedback on their students' writing and averaged 50 responses per paper. The participant who made the most comments actually taught the most students—she taught five classes at two community colleges. The participants' responses included quick notations, such as an added comma, circled capital letter, or crossed-out word. Extensive teaching loads often lend themselves to brief, corrective comments rather than longer, rhetorical comments (Lee, 2009). In a linguistically inclusive grading approach, instructors can reallocate their time to focus on feedback quality over feedback quantity.

To focus on feedback quality, prioritize a set of feedback strategies from a linguistically inclusive approach: Validate and foster the language of Black students; reward linguistic flexibility rather than linguistic assimilation; or use feedback as a conversation. You may want to change your priority from assignment to assignment. Adjust your grading around your chosen priority, reapportioning your time as necessary. Working on just one or two strategies within the set is most feasible (see pp. 120–121).

For example, maybe you may want to focus on communicating high expectations for an assignment. Remember that, in a linguistically inclusive approach, high expectations are coupled with the belief that the student can meet those expectations (Cohen et al., 1999). This new focus may only require reframing what you're already doing. Say your current approach to this particular assignment is to comment on how students can better fulfill the assignment's purpose. In that case, the final comment on a student's paper may look something like this:

> This is a start but you are focused on summarizing rather than synthesizing the sources. Review our notes from class on synthesizing sources and see my comments to revise for a higher grade.

You can maintain this focus on purpose while framing your comments to communicate high expectations:

> I can tell you've taken this assignment seriously. You've taken steps to meet the assignment's purpose but have some work to do on synthesis. I've given comments to help you. This paper has the potential for a higher grade. (adapted from Cohen et al. 1999, p. 1307)

You might also reduce your overall number of comments to only focus on the assignment's primary purpose.

Or, perhaps you want to work on rewarding linguistic flexibility over linguistic assimilation. You might start with the strategy of nonevaluative description. For each paper, you would describe what the student is doing and what you notice about their voice. These can be brief comments:

- Topic sentence sets up the purpose of the paragraph.
- Your word choice contributes to cultivating a conversational voice.
- Your narrative provides a descriptive chronology of events.
- You imply, rather than state, connections among your points.
- I understand your primary purpose to be . . .
- If I had to summarize your paper in one sentence, I would say . . .

Many of these comments do not need to be given in the margins or at specific points. If time necessitates, you can employ this strategy by providing one overall comment on each student's paper.

If you want to use feedback as a conversation, for each paper, aim to ask at least one question that students can answer in class, office hours, or their revisions:

- How does this section relate to your thesis?
- What does your use of "I" do to your argument? How might it strengthen it for some audiences? How might it weaken it for some audiences?
- "Why did you . . .? It's an interesting choice/technique/etc. Why did you choose it?" (Gardner, 1998, para. 5)

Remember that these are not rhetorical questions or corrections phrased as questions. These are questions that you want students to actually answer.

If your students are high-achieving writers, they may expertly apply writing conventions. But remember, the injustice is that many high-achieving students of color sacrifice their voice, language, and identity for writing and academic success. Moreover, students who receive high writing evaluations still deserve quality feedback.

We may not know whether our students are sacrificing their language and identity to achieve in their college writing. That lack of knowledge is one reason a linguistically inclusive grading approach can be so important in such contexts. In particular, it may be most helpful to focus on fostering the language of Black students and rewarding linguistic flexibility over assimilation through audience, purpose, and voice. Strategies to support these goals include references to multiple audiences, peer feedback focused on reader impact, and descriptive comments tying language to purpose, audience(s), and voice. It's also critical to give students the agency to make linguistic decisions. To do so, you may want to tell students directly that they can vary their language on your syllabus and assignment prompts. You might note the following:

- There are many ways for writing to be academic. Think about what you want your voice to sound like.
- You can move away from what we think of as formal writing if doing so better suits your audience and purpose.
- You can use your own language patterns to be an excellent writer.
- I support students in changing the power structure of academic writing.

You can also ask students to consider how they might accomplish rhetorical variation—in your assignment descriptions and your feedback:

- Who are you writing to? Thinking beyond traditional classroom writing, what language and voice might you use to reach your audience?

- Are there any places in this paper where you can go beyond traditional writing conventions to cultivate your voice/reach your audience/achieve your purpose?

If space and time allow, you might combine information about language variation with your strategic questions:

- Traditional academic convention excludes [pattern]. How and why might you challenge this convention for your readers or your voice?

Pronoun choice is one area where students often need instruction in variation. Many college instructors lament that their students have been previously taught to avoid *I*, *we*, and *you* in their writing, contrary to actual academic patterns. You might make comments such as the following:

- It's okay to use *I* in your paper. You did the work, so give yourself credit!
- You can directly address your audience with *you* or *we*.
- How can you connect your academic sources to your own experience?

A linguistically inclusive grading approach can also be helpful for high-achieving students because, unlike with traditional grading approaches, students can learn specifically what makes their writing successful. Regardless of how a student is meeting our expectations, we can and should devote the same amount of thoughtfulness in responding to their work as we do for students who may not be meeting our expectations. In focus groups, Black college students and recent graduates shared their frustration in receiving an A without any explanation of what made the paper an A paper. The absence of feedback made it difficult to determine how to do well on the next assignment. Instead of just a checkmark or a "good work," we can teach through specific positive comments. Remember, such comments can be brief. And even just one or two specific positive comments on a paper can provide students with information to work with on their future writing:

- This stylistic variation between long and short sentences keeps my attention.
- Word choice suits your audience.
- Your narrative provides a descriptive chronology of events.
- I've highlighted some examples of [language pattern]. I can tell that this pattern is part of the voice you are cultivating.

If you teach online asynchronous writing classes, a vital benefit of a linguistically inclusive approach may be feedback as a conversation. For instance, responding to student writing with questions rather than corrections can encourage student interaction with you as the instructor. If you assign multiple drafts, use them as an opportunity to foster this interaction. Assign students to respond to your feedback on their papers as part of the revision process. Online word processors (e.g., Google Docs, Microsoft Word Online) allow multiple users to create and reply to comments without starting a new document. This back-and-forth creates the feeling of conversation, which can be helpful in any teaching context, especially in online asynchronous teaching. When students reply directly to you in the comments, another benefit is immediate access to the context you need, including your original comments, as you grade students' revisions.

To foster conversation through feedback, you can ask questions to help students make their own linguistic choices. In addition to other examples throughout the book, you might ask questions such as the following:

- What do you hope your reader takes away from this question?
- What is your main purpose? Do you want to state your purpose for your audience or have them infer it?
- I highlighted words that give your paper a conversational tone. How do you think this tone suits your audience and purpose?
- "Where do details and specifics stand out? Where does your draft show rather than tell?" (Gardner, 1998, para 5)
- "How would your draft change if you ___?" (Gardner, 1998, para 5)

Again, these questions are posed for students to actually respond to. They are not meant to be corrections but to facilitate students' critical thinking about their writing. Assigning students to respond directly will aid this process.

Reading for student meaning, described in Chapter 3, is another strategy that can set you up for using feedback as a conversation. This strategy is crucial for asynchronous classes where you and the students may have few other chances to clear up any potential misunderstandings. In an online class, once you frame feedback as a conversation, applying the other sets of strategies from a linguistically inclusive grading approach becomes easier. Even without synchronous discussion, you can create feedback interactions that validate the language of Black students, develop metacognition, and explain sociolinguistically informed grading criteria.

If departmental policies limit your grading methods, using sociolinguistic grading criteria and rewarding linguistic flexibility may be tricky. However, you can still validate the language of Black students, use feedback as a conversation, and explain your departmental grading criteria through a linguistically inclusive lens. You can validate the language of Black students by communicating high expectations and pointing out the positive functions of language patterns, such as those of African American English. You can use a sociolinguistic lens to explain departmental grading criteria by contextualizing prescriptive comments and asking questions to help students understand how standards are constructed and reconstructed. It's worth noting that once you become experienced with a linguistically inclusive approach, you can call for needed changes to departmental policies based on what you notice in your students' writing development. With a linguistically inclusive approach, you may see your students engage more with feedback, revise more thoroughly, or think more critically about their writing choices. Because many students are more accustomed to a traditional grading approach—such as plentiful corrections when they don't do well and simply "Great job" when they do—you may even hear words of appreciation from your students about your meaningful comments!

If you use contract grading, know there are many ways to incorporate a linguistically inclusive approach, even without grading individual papers. The strategies you focus on may depend on your particular use of contract grading. Contract grading can provide an excellent opportunity to use feedback as a conversation, especially if your students do not receive grades until the end of the term. If students are comfortable with the grading contract, the lack of grade pressure can help them focus more fully on feedback as a conversation about their writing. Students will feel more comfortable shifting away from aiming for what the instructor wants and toward engaging in their writing development with your supportive feedback. This shift is often one of the goals of contract grading. For you as an instructor, the contract grading method can allow you to more easily read for student meaning rather than judge the quality of a student's writing.

Many grading contracts list criteria for the final class grade. A linguistically inclusive approach can inform these criteria, such as regarding rhetorical variation:

- Transitions reflect your voice and purpose.
- Use of pronouns/person engages your audience.
- Word choice supports informing your audience.
- "The style of the prose speaks to the content, purpose, and audience and is maintained throughout the writing" (Muhammad, 2020, p. 94).
- "The piece is interesting and keeps the reader engaged" (Muhammad, 2020, p. 94).
- The writer uses verb endings with consideration of the rhetorical situation. Specifically, the writer may use African American English-specific verb forms (no endings on verbs with third-person singular subjects such as *it*, *she*, or *he*) OR standardized English verb forms (*–s* endings for verbs with subjects such as *it*, *she*, or *he*) OR both, depending on their audience, purpose, and voice.

Note that these criteria are worded positively, referring to what the student should do or is doing rather than what they should avoid. Explaining to students what they are doing well will support their writing development throughout the class.

In a contract grading model, the formative and other qualitative feedback you provide can use the same linguistically inclusive strategies as noncontract grading methods. You can validate and foster the language of Black students with feedback that describes the positive functions of African American English and descriptive comments that tie students' language use to their purpose and multiple audiences. These comments can support students' metacognition:

- Here, you use African American English patterns that can help engage your readers.
- This phrase emphasizes the point following it.
- What is the impact of the word "really" here?
- This word contributes to a conversational tone.
- This African American English grammar pattern is known as preterit "had" or sometimes innovative "had." It can indicate a pivotal point in a narrative.
- This is a double subject. Double subjects can draw attention to a noun, like a heading. They can also restate complex subjects.

If your students use language patterns beyond African American English and Southern English, you can adapt the approach to their language. If you are unfamiliar with your students' language patterns, you can focus on using feedback as a conversation to learn more about their language variety or varieties. Strategies to support this goal are reading for student meaning, highlighting your subjectivity as a reader, and asking nonevaluative questions about their choices:

- I had to read this sentence a few times to understand it. I think you're saying ____. Do you think this sentence would be better reworded, or do you think your target audience is more familiar with this sentence structure?
- I noticed a switch from past tense to present tense here. Is that intentional? Think about what tense or tenses you want to use and why.

If you are familiar with your students' language patterns, you can focus on rewarding linguistic flexibility over assimilation. The strategies for responding to African American English can be adapted to other language varieties and patterns. The important thing here is to give students both the agency to make linguistic decisions and the information they need to do so. Responses to any language pattern can be framed in this way.

If your students are using generative AI (they are!), a linguistically inclusive approach, and especially linguistically inclusive commenting strategies, can guide your students to think critically about their use of AI. For instance, using feedback as a conversation encourages students to address feedback using the higher levels of Bloom's taxonomy. That is, students often have to analyze, evaluate, or create to respond to strategic questions about their audience, purpose, voice, and linguistic choices—even when AI has made some of these choices. These skills are also the skills that will help students create more effective prompts for AI tools. And if African American English patterns are valued and encouraged in your classroom, it is likely that students will need to go beyond what generative AI offers their writing.

CONCLUSION

I have taught college composition and other writing-intensive classes across disciplines and schools. While I adjusted my pedagogy for each new setting, one thing that stayed consistent was my linguistically inclusive feedback. When students commented on my teaching, they often talked about my feedback on their writing and what they took away from it. In addition to the benefits described throughout the book, a linguistically inclusive grading approach can communicate to students that you care—about their writing development and what they have to say. It was clear that the instructors in my study cared deeply about these things, although their feedback may not have always gotten this message across to their students. Genuine questions, specific commendations, nonevaluative descriptions, and contextualized prescriptive comments let students know that you believe they can meet high expectations and that you will support them in getting there. Of course, many students will continue to read your comments the way they've learned over the years—to figure out how to get a good grade. But they are also likely to grow as writers along the way because the high expectations you set are in part about students making their own writing decisions. Strategies from a linguistically inclusive approach can thus help students understand how seriously you take your role as their writing instructor. Corrections, labels, and general positive comments are much less likely to convey support for students' writing development. In a linguistically inclusive grading approach, instructors foster individual student writers rather than use writing grades for gatekeeping. If grades communicate what we value in writing (O'Neill, 2015; Scott & Inoue, 2015), then a linguistically inclusive grading approach communicates value for Black writers, linguistic diversity, and linguistic agency.

References

Agnew, E. (1997). Cross purposes: Grade deflation, classroom practices. In L. Allison, L. Bryant, & M. Hourigan (Eds.), *Grading in the post-process classroom: From theory to practice* (pp. 36–50). Boynton/Cook.

Alexander, J., Lunsford, K., & Whithaus, C. (2020). Toward wayfinding: A metaphor for understanding writing experiences. *Written Communication, 37*(1), 104–131.

Alim, H. S. (2016). Introducing raciolinguistics: Racing language and languaging race in hyperracial times. In H. S. Alim, J. R. Rickford, & A. E. Ball (Eds.), *Raciolinguistics: How language shapes our ideas about race* (pp. 1–32). Oxford University Press.

Alim, H. S., & Paris, D. (2017). What is culturally sustaining pedagogy and why does it matter? In D. Paris & H. S. Alim (Eds.), *Culturally sustaining pedagogies: Teaching and learning for justice in a changing world* (pp. 1–24). Teachers College Press.

Alston, C. L. (2012). Examining instructional practices, intellectual challenge, and supports for African American student writers. *Research in the Teaching of English, 47*(2), 112–144.

Ambrose, S. A., Bridges, M. W., DiPietro, M., Lovett, M. C., & Norman, M. K. (2010). *How learning works: Seven research-based principles for smart teaching*. Jossey-Bass.

Ampadu, L. (2004). Modeling orality: African American rhetorical practices and the teaching of writing. In E. B. Richardson & R. L. Jackson, II (Eds.), *African American rhetoric(s): Interdisciplinary perspectives* (pp. 136–154). Southern Illinois University Press.

Anderson, L. W., & Krathwohl, D. R. (Eds.). (2001). *A taxonomy for learning, teaching, and assessing: A revision of Bloom's taxonomy of educational objectives*. Longman.

Astin, A. W., & Antonio, A. L. (2012). *Assessment for excellence: The philosophy and practice of assessment and evaluation in higher education* (2nd ed.). Rowman & Littlefield.

Aull, L. (2020). *How students write: A linguistic analysis*. Modern Language Association.

Baker, N. (2014). "Get it off my stack": Teachers' tools for grading papers. *Assessing Writing, 19*(1), 36–50.

Baker-Bell, A. (2017). "I can switch my language but I can't switch my skin:" What teachers must understand about linguistic racism. In E. Moore, A. Michael, & M. W. Penick (Eds.), *The guide for White women who teach Black boys: Understanding, connecting, respecting* (pp. 97–109). SAGE.

Baker-Bell, A. (2020). *Linguistic justice: Black language, literacy, identity, and pedagogy*. NCTE/Routledge.

Baker-Bell, A., Williams-Farrier, B. J., Jackson, D., Johnson, L., Kynard, C., & McMurty, T. (2020). *This ain't another statement! This is a DEMAND for*

Black linguistic justice! Conference on College Composition and Communication. https://cccc.ncte.org/cccc/demand-for-black-linguistic-justice

Balester, V. (2012). How writing rubrics fail: Toward a multicultural model. In A. B. Inoue & M. Poe (Eds.), *Race and writing assessment* (pp. 63–78). Peter Lang.

Ball, A. F. (1992). Cultural preferences and the expository writing of African American adolescents. *Written Communication, 9*(4), 501–532.

Ball, A. F. (1996). Expository writing patterns of African American students. *The English Journal, 85*(1), 27–36.

Ball, A. F. (1999). Evaluating the writing of culturally and linguistically diverse students: The case of the African American vernacular English speaker. In C. R. Cooper & L. Odell (Eds.), *Evaluating writing: The role of teachers' knowledge about text, learning, and culture* (pp. 225–248). National Council of Teachers of English.

Ball, A. F., & Lardner, T. (2005). *African American literacies unleashed: Vernacular English and the composition classroom.* Southern Illinois University Press.

Banks, A. (2005). *Race, rhetoric, and technology: Searching for higher ground.* Taylor & Francis.

Banks, A. (2011). *Digital griots: African American rhetoric in a multimedia age.* Southern Illinois University Press.

Banks, J. A. (2020). Multicultural education: Characteristics and goals. In J. A. Banks & C. A. McGee Banks (Eds.), *Multicultural education: Issues and perspectives* (10th ed., pp. 3–24). John Wiley & Sons.

Barbier. S. (2003). Reflections of "Students' Right to Their Own Language" in first-year composition course objectives and descriptions. *Teaching English in the Two-Year College, 30*(3), 256–267.

Bean, J. C. (2011). *Engaging ideas: The professor's guide to integrating writing, critical thinking, and active learning in the classroom* (2nd ed.). Jossey-Bass.

Behm, N., & Miller, K. D. (2012). Challenging the frameworks of color-blind racism: Why we need a fourth wave of writing assessment scholarship. In A. B. Inoue & M. Poe (Eds.), *Race and writing assessment* (pp. 127–138). Peter Lang.

Behrens, S. (2014). *Understanding language in the classroom: A linguistic guide for college educators.* Multilingual Matters.

Bell, A. (1984). Language style as audience design. *Language in Society, 13*(2), 145–204.

Beneke, M., & Cheatham, G. A. (2015). Speaking up for African American English: Equity and inclusion in early childhood settings. *Early Childhood Education Journal, 43*, 127–134.

Biber, D., Nekrasova, T., & Horn, B. (2011). *The effectiveness of feedback for L1-English and L2-writing development: A meta-analysis.* ETS.

Bishop, L. (2023). A computer wrote this paper: What ChatGPT means for education, research, and writing. *Social Science Research Network.* https://ssrn.com/abstract=4338981, http://doi.org/10.2139/ssrn.4338981

Blake, R. (2016). Toward heterogeneity: A sociolinguistic perspective on the classification of Black people in the twenty-first century. In H. S. Alim, J. R. Rickford, & A. E. Ball (Eds.), *Raciolinguistics: How language shapes our ideas about race* (pp. 153–170). Oxford University Press.

Bloom, B. S., Engelhart, M. D., Furst, E. J., Hill, W. H., & Krathwohl, D. R. (1956). *Taxonomy of educational objectives: The classification of educational goals.* Handbook I: Cognitive domain. David McKay Company.

Boyd, R. (1998). The origins and evolution of grading student writing: Pedagogical imperatives and cultural anxieties. In F. Zak & C. C. Weaver (Eds.), *The theory and practice of grading writing: Problems and possibilities* (pp. 3–16). State University of New York Press.

Broad, B. (2003). *What we really value: Beyond rubrics in teaching and assessing writing*. Utah State University Press.

Burns (née Wise), A. & Franz, H. (née: Askin). (2009). *Composition instruction at North Carolina State University: An exploratory study*. South Eastern Conference on Linguistics, New Orleans, LA.

Calhoun, K., Charity Hudley, A. H., Bucholtz, M., Exford, J., & Johnson, B. (2021). Attracting Black students to linguistics through a Black-centered introduction to linguistics course. *Language, 97*(1), 1–26.

Charity Hudley, A. H. (2017). Language and racialization. In O. Garcia, N. Flores, & M. Spotti (Eds.), *The Oxford handbook of language and society* (pp. 381–402). Oxford University Press.

Charity Hudley, A. H., Dickter, C., & Franz, H. (2017). *The indispensable guide to undergraduate research: Success in and beyond college*. Teachers College Press.

Charity Hudley, A. H., & Mallinson, C. (2011). *Understanding English language variation in U.S. schools*. Teachers College Press.

Charity Hudley, A. H., & Mallinson, C. (2014). *We do language: English language variation in the secondary English classroom*. Teachers College Press.

Charity Hudley, A. H., & Mallinson, C. (2019). Linguistic society of America statement on race. https://www.linguisticsociety.org/content/lsa-statement-race

Charity Hudley, A. H., Mallinson, C., & Bucholtz, M. (2022). *Talking college*. Teachers College Press.

Cohen, G. L., Steele, C. M., & Ross, L. D. (1999). The mentor's dilemma: Providing critical feedback across the racial divide. *Personality and Social Psychology Bulletin, 25*(10), 1302–1318.

Coleman, T. J., DeLong, R., DeVore, K. S., Gibney, S., & Kuhne, M. C. (2016). The risky business of engaging racial equity in writing instruction: A tragedy in five acts. *Teaching English in the Two-Year College, 43*(4), 347–370.

Conference on College Composition and Communication. (1974). Students' right to their own language. *College Composition and Communication, 25*, 1–18.

Connors, R. J. (1986). Textbooks and the evolution of the discipline. *College Composition and Communication, 37*(2), 178–194.

Cox, R. (2009). *The college fear factor: How students and professors misunderstand one another*. Harvard University Press.

Crowley, S. (1998). *Composition in the university: Historical and polemical essays*. University of Pittsburgh Press.

Delpit, L. (1988). The silenced dialogue: Power and pedagogy in educating other people's children. *Harvard Educational Review, 58*(3), 280–298.

Delpit, L. (2006). *Other people's children: Cultural conflict in the classroom*. The New Press.

Delpit, L. (2012). *"Multiplication is for white people": Raising expectations for other people's children*. The New Press.

Dixson, A. D., & Rousseau Anderson, C. K. (2017). Critical race theory and education: Singing a "new" song. In A. D. Dixon, C. K. Rosseau Anderson, & J. K. Donnor (Eds.), *Critical race theory in education: All God's children got a song* (2nd ed., pp. 1–8). Routledge.

Edim, G. (2018). *Well-read Black girl: Finding our stories, discovering ourselves.* Ballantine Books.

Fasching-Varner, K. (2009). No! The team ain't alright! The institutional and individual problematics of race. *Social Identities, 15*(6), 811–829.

Finley, A. (2021). *How college contributes to workforce success: Employer views on what matters most.* Association of American Colleges and Universities.

Fogarty, M. (2015). When to use an apostrophe. *Quick and dirty tips.* https://www.quickanddirtytips.com/articles/when-to-use-an-apostrophe/.

Fogarty, M. (2016). Affect versus effect. *Quick and dirty tips.* https://www.quickanddirtytips.com/articles/affect-versus-effect/

Franz, H. (2016). *Access to college-ready writing through classroom writing assessment.* Literacy Research Association Annual Conference, Nashville, TN.

Franz, H. (2019). *Instructor response to language variation in community college composition papers.* Proquest Dissertations and Theses database.

Franz, H., Charity Hudley, A. H., Rowell, A., Johnson, S. J., Tano, M., & Grue, M. P. (2021). *Students' right to their own writing: Guides for undergraduate research and for college student writers and their instructors.* www.srtow.org

Franz, H., Charity Hudley, A. H., Rowell, A., Johnson, S. J., Tano, M., & Grue, M. P. (2022). Black students' linguistic agency: An evidenced-based guide for instructors and students. *American Speech, 97*(2), 230–247.

Franz, H., Grue, M. P., Rowell, A., Tano, M., Johnson, S. J., & Charity Hudley, A. H. (in press). Black linguistic justice from theory to practice. *College Composition and Communication.*

Gaither, S. E., Cohen-Goldberg, A. M., Gidney, C. L., & Maddox, K. B. (2015). Sounding Black or White: Priming identity and biracial speech. *Frontiers in Psychology, 6.*

Gardner, T. (1998). *Traci's 4th list of ten: Ten ways to respond to student drafts.* http://www.tengrrl.com/tens/004.shtml

Gareis, C., & Grant, L. (2015). *Teacher-made assessments: How to connect curriculum, instruction, and student learning* (2nd ed.). Routledge.

Gere, A. R., Swofford, S. C., Silver, N., & Pugh, M. (2015). Interrogating disciplines/disciplinarity in WAC/WID: An institutional study. *College Composition and Communication, 67*(2), 243–266.

Gilyard, K., & Richardson, E. (2001). Students' right to possibility: Basic writing and African American rhetoric. In A. Greenbaum (Ed.), *Insurrection: Approaches to resistance in composition studies* (pp. 37–51). SUNY Press.

Giovanni, N. (2007). *Acolytes.* HarperCollins.

Grammarly Inc. (2023). *Grammarly premium.* https://app.grammarly.com/

Green, L. (2002). *African American English: A linguistic introduction.* Cambridge University Press.

Grieve, J. (2016). *Regional variation in written American English.* Cambridge University Press.

Grue, M. P. (2020). Literacy narrative rubric. https://charityhudleydickterfranz.com/instructor-guide-types-of-grading-feedback-and-revision/#Rubric_Checklist_Categories

Hankerson, S. (2017). Black voices matter. *Language Arts Journal of Michigan, 32*(2), 34–39.

Helmbrecht, B. (2007). Giving grades, taking tolls: Assessing the impact of evaluation on developing writers. *Teaching English in the Two-Year College, 34*(3), 306–319.

Himley, M., & Carini, P. F. (2000). *From another angle: Children's strengths and school standards: The Prospect Center's descriptive review of the child* (p. 230). Teachers College Press.

Horner, B. (1996). Discoursing basic writing. *College Composition and Communication, 47*(2), 199–222.

Inoue, A. B. (2014). A grade-less writing course that focuses on labor and assessing. In D. Coxwell-Teague & R. F. Lunsford (Eds.), *First-year composition: From theory to practice* (pp. 71–110). Parlor Press.

Inoue, A. B. (2015). *Antiracist writing assessment ecologies: Teaching and assessing writing for a socially just future.* The WAC Clearinghouse.

Jeffery, F., & Selting, B. (1999). Reading the invisible ink: Assessing the responses of non-composition faculty. *Assessing Writing*, *6*(2), 179–197.

Kates, S. (2001). *Activist rhetorics and American higher education 1885–1937.* Southern Illinois University Press.

Kimball, D., & Jazzar, M. (2011, April 14). To increase learner achievement serve feedback sandwiches. https://www.facultyfocus.com/articles/teaching-and-learning/to-increase-learner-achievement-serve-feedback-sandwiches/

King, Martin Luther, Jr. (1965). *How long? Not long.* https://voicesofdemocracy.umd.edu/dr-martin-luther-king-jr-long-not-long-speech-text/

Konold, H. E., Miller, S. P., & Konold, K. B. (2004). Using teacher feedback to enhance student learning. *Teaching Exceptional Children, 36*(6), 64–69.

Kuh, G. (2008). *High-impact educational practices: What they are, who has access to them, and why they matter.* Association of American Colleges & Universities.

Kynard, C. (2007). "Wanted: Some Black long distance [writers]": Blackboard Flava-Flavin and other AfroDigital experiences in the classroom. *Computers and Composition, 24*, 329–345.

Kynard, C. (2013). *Vernacular insurrections: Race, Black protest, and the new century in composition-literacy studies.* SUNY Press.

Ladson-Billings, Gloria. (2009). *The dreamkeepers.* Jossey-Bass.

Learn Prompting. (2023). Introductory course on generative AI and prompt engineering. https://learnprompting.org/docs/intro

Lee, J. W. (2016). Beyond translingual writing. *College English, 79*(2), 174–195.

Lee, M. (2009). Rhetorical roulette: Does writing-faculty overload disable effective response to student writing? *Teaching English in the Two-Year College, 37*(2), 165–177.

Lippi-Green, R. (2012). *English with an accent: Language, ideology, and discrimination in the United States* (2nd ed.). Routledge.

Looker, S. (2016). Writing about language: Studying language diversity with first-year writers. *Teaching English in the Two-Year College, 44*(2), 176–198.

Lopatto, D. (2007). Undergraduate research experiences support science career decisions and active learning. *CBE Life Sciences Education, 6*, 297–306.

Lunsford, A. A., & Lunsford, K. J. (2008). "Mistakes are a fact of life": A national comparative study. *College Composition and Communication, 59*(4), 781–806.

Matarese, M. T., & Anson, C. (2010). Teacher response to AAE features in the writing of college students: A case study in the social construction of error. In J. B. Smith (Ed.), *The elephant in the classroom: Race and writing* (pp. 111–136). Hampton University Press.

Matsuda, P. K. (2006). The myth of linguistic homogeneity in U.S. college composition. *College English, 68*(6), 637–651.

McMurty, T. (2023). "Changing the course of the stream": A retrospective analysis of artful language learning opportunities. *Journal of Adolescent and Adult Literacy, 67*(2), 74–84.

Mosher, S. B. (2020). Ideology, expectation, and evaluation: How linguistic experiences and attitudes inform response to AAE-strong student writing. *Pedagogy, 20*(30), 431–452.

Muhammad, G. (2020). *Cultivating genius: An equity framework for culturally and historically responsive literacy.* Scholastic.

Muiru, K. (2021). Black language in children's and YA lit. *Black Language Syllabus.* http://www.blacklanguagesyllabus.com/black-language-in-childrens—ya-lit.html

Myers, J. C., & Kircher, C. (2007). Teaching without license: Outsider perspectives on first-year writing. *Teaching English in the Two-Year College, 34*(4), 396–404.

National Center for Education Statistics. (2016). Post-bachelor's employment outcomes by sex and race/ethnicity. *The Condition of Education.*

National Research Council. (2000). *How people learn: Brain, mind, experience, and school: Expanded edition.* The National Academies Press.

Naynaha, S. (2016). Assessment, social justice, and Latinxs in the US community college. *College English, 9*(2), 1996–201.

Okonkwo, T. M. (2021). Black rhetoric. *Black Language Syllabus.* http://www.blacklanguagesyllabus.com/black-rhetoric.html

O'Neill, P. (2015). Threshold concepts at the crossroads: Writing instruction and assessment. In L. Adler-Kassner & E. Wardle (Eds.), *Naming what we know: Threshold concepts of writing studies* (pp. 157–170). Utah State University Press.

OpenAI. (2023). ChatGPT (July 25 version) [Large language model]. https://chat.openai.com/chat

Paris, D. (2012). Culturally sustaining pedagogy: A needed change in stance, terminology, and practice. *Educational Researcher, 41*(3), 93–97.

Perryman-Clark, S. M. (2012). Africanized patterns of expression: A case study of African American students' expository writing patterns across written contexts. *Pedagogy: Critical Approaches to Teaching Literature, Language, Composition, and Culture, 12*(2), 253–280.

Perryman-Clark, S. M. (2013a). African American language, rhetoric, and students' writing: New directions for SRTOL. *College Composition and Communication, 64*(3), 469–495.

Perryman-Clark, S. M. (2013b). *Afrocentric teacher-research: Rethinking appropriateness and inclusion.* Peter Lang.

Perryman-Clark, S. M. (2016). Who we are(n't) assessing: Racializing language and writing assessment in writing program administration. *College English, 79*(2), 206–211.

Poe, M., Elliot, N., Cogan, J. A. J., & Nurudeen, T. G. J. (2014). The legal and the local: Using disparate impact analysis to understand the consequences of writing assessment. *College Composition and Communication, 65*(4), 588–611.

Porter, C. (1999). *Imani all mine.* Houghton Mifflin.

Purdue Online Writing Lab (OWL). (2022). Creating your persona. https://owl.purdue.edu/owl/general_writing/writing_style/style%20/creating_personas.html

Redd, T. (1995). Untapped resources: "Styling" in Black students' writing for Black audiences. In D. L. Rubin (Ed.), *Composing social identity in written language* (pp. 221–240). Lawrence Erlbaum Associates.

Redd, T. M., & Webb, K. S. (2005). *A teacher's introduction to African American English: What a writing teacher should know.* Teachers College Press.
Richardson, E. (2000). Critique on the problematic of implementing Afrocentricity into traditional curriculum: "The powers that be." *Journal of Black Studies, 31*(2), 196–213.
Richardson, E. (2003). *African American literacies.* Routledge.
Rickford, J. R., & Rickford, R. J. (2000). *Spoken soul: The story of Black English.* John Wiley & Sons.
Rose, M. (1985). The language of exclusion: Writing instruction at the university. *College English, 47*(4), 341–359.
Royster, J. J. (2002). Academic discourses or small boats on a big sea. In C. Schroeder, H. Fox, & P. Bizzell (Eds.), *Alt dis: Alternative discourses and the academy* (pp. 23–30). Boynton/Cook.
Royster, J. J., & Williams, J. C. (1999). History in the spaces left: African American presence and narratives of composition studies. *College Composition and Communication, 50*(4), 563–584.
Russel, D. R. (2006). Historical studies of composition. In P. Smagorinsky (Ed.). *Research on composition, 1983–2003* (pp. 243–273). Teachers College Press.
Savani, C. (2021). Ten ways to tackle linguistic bias in our classrooms. *Inside Higher Ed.* https://www.insidehighered.com/advice/2021/01/27/how-professors-can-and-should-combat-linguistic-prejudice-their-classes-opinion?fbclid=IwAR1Vn3suthW8ksbB5anaV0Nz6Pq71lM-lu9Hzvp_2BI7y63h9gBJQnmT-kk
Schneider, B. (2005). Dialect and the discourse of evaluation. In P. Bruch & R. Marbach (Eds.), *The hope and the legacy: The past, present, and future of "Students' right to their own language"* (pp. 195–212). Hampton Press.
Scott, B., & Inoue, A. B. (2015). Assessing writing shapes contexts and instruction. In L. Adler-Kassner & E. Wardle (Eds.), *Naming what we know: Threshold concepts of writing studies* (pp. 29–31). Utah State University Press.
Shapiro, R., & Del Russo, C. (2023). Working toward racial justice in the writing center: Five strategies for translingual tutoring. In T. Haltiwanger Morrison & D. A. Evans Garriott (Eds.), *Writing centers and racial justice: A guidebook for critical praxis* (pp. 120–138). University Press of Colorado.
Shaughnessy, M. (1977). *Errors and expectations: A guide for the teacher of basic writing.* Oxford University Press.
Shute, V. (2008). Focus on formative feedback. *Review of Educational Research, 78*(1), 153–189.
Smallwood, M. L. (1935). *An historical study of examinations and grading systems in early American universities. Harvard studies in education Vol. 24.* Harvard University Press.
Smith, B. (2023). Against the writing center. *Chronicle of Higher Education.* https://www.chronicle.com/article/against-the-writing-center?utm_source=Iterable&utm_medium=email&utm_campaign=campaign_5865730_nl_Academe-Today_date_20230105&cid=at&source=&sourceid=&cid2=gen_login_refresh
Smith, P. (2019). "How does a Black person speak English?" Beyond American language norms. *American Educational Research Journal, 57*(1), 106–147.
Smitherman, G. (1977). *Talkin and testifyin: The language of Black America.* Houghton Mifflin.
Smitherman, G. (1994). "The blacker the berry, the sweeter the juice": African American student writers. In A. H. Dyson & C. Genishi (Eds.), *The need for*

story: Cultural diversity in classroom and community (pp. 80–101). National Council of Teachers of English.

Sonnenmoser, R. (2009). The gatekeeping impulse and Professor X: An exploration. *Assessing Writing, 14*(2), 76–87.

St. Mary's University of Minnesota Writing Assessment Rubric. (2008). St. Mary's University of Minnesota.

Stern, L. A., & Solomon, A. (2006). Effective faculty feedback: The road less traveled. *Assessing Writing, 11*, 22–41.

Students for Fair Admissions, Inc. v. President and Fellows of Harvard College, 600 U.S. ___ (2023).

Sword, H. (2012). *Stylish academic writing.* Harvard University Press.

Terry, O. K. (2023, May 12). I'm a student: You have no idea how much we're using ChatGPT. *Chronicle of Higher Education.* https://www.chronicle.com/article/im-a-student-you-have-no-idea-how-much-were-using-chatgpt?utm_source=Iterable&utm_medium=email&utm_campaign=campaign_6893319_nl_Academe-Today_date_20230524&cid=at&source=&sourceid=

Thomas, A. (2017). *The Hate U Give.* Balzer + Bray.

Tieje, R., Sutcliffe, E., Hillebrand, H., & Buchen, W. (1915). Systematizing grading in freshman composition at the large university. *The English Journal, 4*(9), 586–597.

Trimbur, J. (1996). Response: Why do we test writing? In E. M. White, W. D. Lutz, & S. Kamusikiri (Eds.), *Assessment of writing: Politics, policies, practices* (pp. 45–48). Modern Language Association of America.

Very Smart Brothas. (2023). *The Root.* https://www.theroot.com/very-smart-brothas

Veysey, L. (1965). *The emergence of the American university.* University of Chicago Press.

Villanueva, V. (2001). The politics of literacy across the curriculum. In S. H. McLeod, E. Miraglia, M. Soven, & C. Thaiss (Eds.), *WAC for the new millennium: Strategies for continuing writing-across-the-curriculum programs* (pp. 165–178). National Council of Teachers of English.

Williams-Farrier, B. (2013). Students' "write" to their own language: Teaching the African American verbal tradition as a rhetorically effective writing skill. *Equity & Excellence in Education, 46*(3), 411–429.

Winograd, G., & Rust, J. P. (2014). Stigma, awareness of support services, and academic help-seeking among historically underrepresented first-year college students. *The Learning Assistance Review, 19*(2), 17.

Woodson, C. G. (1990). *The miseducation of the Negro.* Winston-Derek. (Original work published 1933)

Writer's Choice Grammar and Composition Writing Assessment and Evaluation Rubrics Grade 12. (2008). Glencoe/McGraw Hill.

Young, V. A. (2010). Should writers use they own English? *Iowa Journal of Cultural Studies, 12*(1), 110–118.

Young, V. A., Barret, R., Young-Rivera, Y.S., Lovejoy, K. B. (2018). Other people's English: Code-meshing, code-switching, and African American literacy. Parlor Press.

Young, V. A., & Young-Rivera, Y. S. (2013). It ain't what it is: Code-switching and White American celebrationists. *JAC, 33*(1/2), 396–401.

Zaluda, S. (1998). Lost voices of the Harlem renaissance: Writing assigned at Howard University, 1919–31. *College Composition and Communication, 50*(2), 232–257.

Index

Note: Page numbers followed by *f* or *t* indicate material in figures or tables respectively.

About the Author

Hannah Franz is the program associate for graduate advisement at the Jack Kent Cooke Foundation. She holds a Ph.D. in educational leadership from the College of William & Mary, an M.S.Ed. in reading/writing/literacy from the University of Pennsylvania, and an M.A. in linguistics from North Carolina State University. She is a coauthor of *The Indispensable Guide to Undergraduate Research: Success in and Beyond College* (Teachers College Press) with Anne Charity Hudley and Cheryl Dickter. Hannah has taught writing, linguistics, and education courses at Virginia Commonwealth University, Reynolds Community College, and the College of William & Mary.